UNDERCURRENTS

Prison Policy in Ireland:
Criminal Justice versus Social Justice

UNDERCURRENTS

Other titles in the series

UNDERCURRENTS   Series Editor Carol Coulter

Prison Policy in Ireland: Criminal Justice versus Social Justice

PAUL O'MAHONY

CORK UNIVERSITY PRESS

First published in 2000 by
Cork University Press
University College
Cork
Ireland

© Paul O'Mahony 2000

British Library Cataloguing in Publication Data
A CIP catalogue record for this book is available from
the British Library

ISBN 1 85918 243 7

Typeset by Tower Books, Ballincollig, Co. Cork
Printed by ColourBooks Ltd., Baldoyle, Co. Dublin

Contents

Acknowledgements

I would like to acknowledge the cheerful support of Alan McCrea, Myrtle and Sheila Greene and Kit and Helen O'Mahony.

Paul O'Mahony,
March, 2000

Introduction

This pamphlet sets out to describe exactly how and why the Irish prison system presents a serious challenge to the ordinary Irish citizen as well as to the Minister for Justice and the newly appointed Director of Prisons. That the system has many serious problems of various kinds has been obvious to all for many years, but it is more difficult to convince the ordinary citizen that the character of the penal system is one of the key indicators of the general health of Irish society and therefore very much his or her business. The Irish people have an obvious interest in the reduction of crime, but they should also have a strong interest in the manner in which the state inflicts punishment on offenders in their name. Indeed, public interest should be far more acute than it is, in part because of the overwhelming evidence, which will be adduced in this pamphlet, that the Irish penal system is not only ineffective at reducing crime, but likely in many cases to foster it.

There are other more principled, less expedient reasons for the citizen to be concerned with the prisons. There is the irrefutable evidence of inhumane, degrading conditions in some Irish prisons. There is the dire lack of therapeutic and rehabilitative services for the many prisoners with severe personal problems. There is the absurd use of prison – the ultimate weapon in the state's armoury of coercion – against petty offenders, juveniles and fine-defaulters. But this pamphlet will also attempt to relate these various problems to an underlying malaise: the almost entirely negative role the system plays in the construction of a more just social order. This is, arguably, the most serious crisis of the criminal justice and penal system.

David Garland[1] has suggested that: 'The infliction of punishment by a state upon its citizens bears the character of a civil war in miniature – it depicts a society engaged in a struggle with itself'. Prison is frequently understood as a response to individuals who choose to flout society's rules, but Garland's use of the metaphor of civil war reminds us that in Ireland the prison is used to a hugely disproportionate extent to suppress miscreants

1

from the lowest echelons of society. It is hardly ever used against the powerful and privileged, who are prone to commit a different, but equally damaging, type of crime. The case will be made that the benefits and costs of the penal system must be measured not just in economic terms, or by its success at crime reduction, but also with regard to its wider implications for the quality and justice of Irish society as a whole.

As long ago as 1985, the Whitaker Committee[2] recognised the significant contribution of social deprivation and disadvantage to the creation of crime. The committee argued that 'it is clearly not by any reform of the criminal justice system, but rather by more wide-ranging economic and social policies, that the problem of juvenile crime can be tackled.' This pamphlet, while agreeing with the Committee's emphasis on the importance of tackling structural inequalities in the economic and social system, takes issue with the implication that the criminal justice system itself is not amenable to reform (with the potential to impact positively on social justice). The case will be made that there are many aspects of the criminal justice and penal system that can and should be reformed primarily for the sake of greater social justice. It will also be argued that a more genuinely egalitarian society cannot be achieved without first achieving reform of the criminal justice and penal system.

This pamphlet is timely because after several decades of chaotic growth (by and large unrelated to the growth in serious crime), rudderless management, deteriorating conditions and services, and political and bureaucratic neglect, the government has decided to pour substantial resources into the prison system and establish an Independent Prisons Board to oversee its administration. There is, therefore, a potent opportunity to get to grips with the problems of the criminal justice and penal system and to turn the system round. On the other hand, there must be a real fear that the on-going massive expansion of the system, to almost double its 1996 capacity, will, in the absence of a genuinely reforming new approach, simply double the woes and the negative social impact of the system. Ireland has recently become uncomfortably aware of its past failure at the work of creating safe, caring, ethical institutions for children in need. While prisoners are obviously less sympathetic subjects for concern, it is clear that critical appraisal of the failures of Irish penal institutions is now long overdue and that continued neglect of these problems would be inexcusable.

1. Defining the prisons problem

All too frequently we hear that the prison system is in crisis, but nevertheless the system trundles on, indifferent to all criticism – a seemingly necessary and basically unchanging evil in modern Irish society. Perhaps the real crisis is that the only political and public attention given to the prison system is the short-lived concern stimulated by intermittent disasters that tend to be hyped by the media, like escapes, suicides, and administrative errors. The most recent example of this is the Sheedy case, which has led to the resignation of a High Court and a Supreme Court Judge and a senior court official. At the centre of this controversy, which is focused on possible abuse of judicial power, was the procedurally irregular, early release by the courts, in late 1998, of a middle-class person sentenced to four years for manslaughter while drunk-driving. This case has raised extremely important issues about the impartiality of the judiciary and the putative, intrinsic bias of the Irish penal system in favour of the more powerful and privileged members of society, but, as always, the main media and public interest has been on the political fall-out rather than on how the criminal justice system is structured and actually operates.

In his preface to the second edition of the book *I Did Penal Servitude* by Prisoner Number D83222 (1946),[3] Sean O'Faolain wrote: 'We [the Irish] are not a thoughtless people, but we are an unthinking people: we begin to think only when our feelings are deeply moved, and if anyone can read these pages without being profoundly stirred he is about the only sort of person whom I would be genuinely glad to see put in prison.' More than fifty years on, Irish society's response to the prison system is still dominated by occasional, fleeting reactions to emotive, human-interest stories and politically focused debacles. Unfortunately, this voyeuristic, scandal-hunting inclination co-exists with a smug indifference to the routine, grinding failure and misery of the everyday prison system.

There are numerous valid, if sometimes competing, standpoints from which to judge the penal system and assess its merits and failings. One might mention the perspectives of the victim of crime, of the imprisoned offender, of the ordinary concerned citizen, of those with political power and responsibility, of the social theorist and of the professional workers in law and law enforcement or custodial and rehabilitation services. Inevitably, however, the standpoint of the administration tends to monopolise debate and set the practical agenda.

The current ideological preoccupation of the Irish prisons administration is with what might be called *enlightened managerialism* – the application of modern business management techniques to the running of the penal system, leavened with a sense of social conscience. The Government and its civil service bureaucracy see themselves as charged primarily with the effective management of a penal system, which is, in their view, largely shaped by forces outside their control. The main focus of managerialism in the prisons is on standard-setting and the achievement of cost-effectiveness in the implementation of what is seen as the difficult but necessary community service of punishment by the state in the name of the people.

This modern managerialist outlook can be called enlightened to the extent that it defines its task in relation to a framework of humane, socially acceptable and politically desirable objectives. For example, *The Management of Offenders: a Five Year Plan*,[4] the first major official document on prison policy in the history of the state, describes the main overall aims of the prison system as a) to provide and operate an efficient, effective and just prison system and b) to contain in custody those members of the community committed to prison by the courts, all the while promoting the physical and mental well-being of those in custody and preparing them to resume a constructive place in the community on their release. This document states that the first principle governing imprisonment is that prisoners are sent to prison *as* punishment not *for* punishment and that they should 'suffer no hardship greater than that which is inherent in the deprivation of liberty'. There is also a commitment in the Five Year Plan to 'treat those in custody with care, justice, dignity and respect and make available to them such help, guidance, counselling, education and training as will lead them, as far as practicable, to a constructive life in the community on release'.

These aims and objectives are not only unobjectionable but are lucid, civilised and worthy. They are based on a seemingly principled concern with justice and on an explicit commitment to positive, rehabilitative interventions on behalf of prisoners. It might appear, then, that all that is required for a thorough assessment of the Irish prison system and a diagnosis of its problems is an examination of the reality of the prison system and careful measurement of the extent to which it lives up to its own declared goals. While such an examination is necessary and, as we will see, profoundly disappointing and disturbing, it is clearly a mistake to assume that the problem of imprisonment begins and ends with the system's success or failure at meeting its own targets – however benevolent and justifiable they might appear to be.

There are two main difficulties with restricting the prison problem to the issue of management efficiency and cost-effectiveness in achieving the goals laid down by *The Management of Offenders: a Five Year Plan*. First, such an approach is far too narrow because the administration's goals, although worthy and sensible, reflect an uncritical acceptance of the criminal justice system as it presently stands. The prison system's task is defined, by the administration, to start at the point when individuals are committed by the courts to serve a sentence. What crime is and the pressing need to suppress and reduce it are taken for granted. The whole process by which crime is constructed and by which certain offenders are selected for the last resort sanction of imprisonment is taken as an unquestionable given.

This is clearly inadequate since it is possible, indeed necessary, to ask what purposes the prison system serves in society over and above the purposes claimed for individual instances of imprisonment. Émile Durkheim[5], for example, argued that crime is functional for society to such a degree that, if it did not exist, it would have to be invented. This is because the concept of crime and a criminal class and the perceived need to mobilise the forces of the state against crime have major beneficial effects for social cohesion. They promote the credibility of the state as an entity, the legitimacy of its powerful agencies and agents, and the conformity of the generality of people to mainstream values. These ideas raise the interesting possibility that the penal system survives and takes the form it does, mainly because of its effects on the general population and on the social system as a whole, rather than because it has any useful or justifiable impact on individuals punished by imprisonment.

Michel Foucault[6], indeed, interprets the penological failure of the prison as a deliberate political strategy. He has proposed that the prison is in fact, at this level, not a failure at all but, on the contrary, a well-disguised success. Prison, in other words, succeeds at entirely different tasks to its ostensible aim of crime control. According to Foucault, the true underlying function of prison is not to control the criminal 'so much as to control the working class by creating the criminal'. The interlocking facts that Irish prisoners generally have a profile of extreme relative social disadvantage and that many types of serious crime, committed by the more privileged Irish classes, are not punished by imprisonment, or even punished at all, indicate that Foucault's notion is far from an exotic, intellectual conceit.

The prison system is obviously part of a wider criminal justice system and cannot be properly understood outside of this context. Furthermore, the criminal justice system itself is only the most explicit and formal system of social control among many other such systems that exist in society in order to distribute, manage, and exert power. The criminal justice system and the prison system represent the state's routine exercise of its monopoly on legitimate violence, but this use of power is inescapably enmeshed in other power relations within society. How power is exercised over individuals in prison is of central importance, but the wider role of prisons can only be grasped and properly evaluated in relation to the general exercise of social, economic and political power.

Second, history and experience teach us that penal authorities and administrations have always had a positive and seemingly principled rationale for their system of imprisonment, however brutal, ineffective and dehumanising it might be. They have always had a superficially persuasive, self-legitimising rhetoric. Even the obscene, unspeakably brutal regime that governed the Auschwitz concentration camp had the temerity to place over the entrance to the camp the savagely ironic slogan 'Arbeit macht frei' (work brings freedom). To set out to examine a system by measuring how far it falls short of its own objectives, however worthy they might appear, is insufficient and potentially a mere distraction. It is too easy an approach because it avoids the more fundamental question about why prison systems seem to be structured so as to inevitably fail at realising their own, supposedly cherished goals. It does not confront the possibility that there are other deeply ingrained, but suppressed and less worthy, goals that effectively subvert the publicly declared goals.

The great paradox of prisons lies in their capacity for harm, their tendency not only to fail to improve matters, but often to make things much worse. How, as systems, can prisons endure, indeed expand and in some ways flourish, despite their evident futility and the damage they cause? The gap between the cosy, present-day managerial rhetoric, with its seemingly benign interest in the welfare of prisoners, and the reality of life for many prisoners, is so vast that it would be a grave error to assume that the right principles are in place and that we need only ensure that these principles are put into practice. The alarming possibility exists that in some way or other the official expression of fine principles is not only an as yet unfulfilled aspiration but, far more sinisterly, is also a means by which the discreditable *status quo* of the prison system is enabled to persist and evade the radical reconstruction that it so desperately requires.

Statements of intent in the area of criminal justice are fraught with difficulty and should not always be taken at face value. It is right and proper for our system to be directed by explicit, humane, positive objectives, but there is a serious problem when such statements of intent are one-dimensional and fail to acknowledge the possibly successful, covert mission of the prison and the more negative objectives of imprisonment, which are intrinsic to our present system and, perhaps, an ineradicable part of it.

Examine, for example, the proclaimed first principle of our system – that prisoners are sent to prison *as* punishment not *for* punishment. This is obviously a key statement, establishing an ethos that disallows a whole range of behaviours within Irish penal institutions. It declares categorically and unequivocally that prisoners are not to receive harsh, punitive treatment within the system. Penal servitude, physical rigours, corporal punishment, psychological and emotional pressure and deprivations of all kinds are clearly prohibited by this statement. The punishment to be inflicted is solely the deprivation of liberty and the strictures and loss of rights that are an unavoidable consequence of this deprivation. Read in this manner, and no doubt this is how it is intended to be read, the statement is a crucial and highly valuable prescription for the prison system, a statement of the kind of core values that might underpin a humane and constructive prison system – in which there is no place for vengeance, recrimination, humiliation and degradation.

On the other hand, even the slightest acquaintance with the actual conditions of our prisons makes it abundantly clear that the statement that prisoners are sent to prison *as* punishment not *for* punishment is a flagrant nonsense. As Pat Carlen[7] asks: if this principle is so energetically and faithfully upheld, 'how is it prisons are not more like three star hotels?' Carlen answers her own query with the assertion that 'when prison-induced pains are recognised, they are usually depicted as being regrettable but inevitable adjuncts of enforced confinement . . . they are not evaluated as the carefully-achieved products of a most cherished site of state punishment.'

The experience of imprisonment in Ireland is punitive, damaging and painful in a myriad of ways beyond the mere loss of liberty and, in many quarters, it is expected to be so. The reality of prisons is not only remote from the noble sentiment that prisoners should suffer only deprivation of liberty and no further punishment, it makes a mockery of it. For many prisoners, the conditions and regimes they experience are brutal, dangerous and demeaning – a nightmare world of insanitary, overcrowded, threatening, depersonalising, disease-ridden and drug-infested horrors. As Carol Coulter[8] has documented, the web of punishment also extends beyond the prisoner and beyond the prison to entangle innocent wives, parents and children. Stigmatisation, alienation and lack of social support also ensure that punishment will continue even after the prisoner regains his[9] precious but often, socially and economically, very circumscribed liberty. The prison problem, then, though deeply concerned with, is very definitely not restricted to, the question of what happens to people after they arrive in prison.

The state's declared philosophy and objectives for the prisons are premised on the view that the prisons can be dealt with as a self-contained subsystem. This approach presupposes the legitimacy of the society and criminal justice system that feeds in prisoners. The state's expressed philosophy and objectives are of the utmost importance and the extent to which the system conforms to its own standards and realises its own objectives is obviously a matter of profound concern. But, while, for example, the internal justice and humanity of the prisons, conceived as an isolated subsystem, are vital, there are equally vital questions of justice and legitimacy, which require us to make links between the prison system and the operation of wider society. For instance, who is sent to prison and why and who avoids prison, despite breaking the criminal law, are questions that interrogate Irish social, political and cultural values and not just the criminal justice process and penal system. The state's philosophy and objectives for the prisons need to be scrutinised for their more fundamental validity and viability, as well as for the effectiveness of their implementation. It may even emerge that they involve serious contradictions and represent an ultimately untenable stance. The chasm between the strong humanitarian rhetoric of the system and the reality of prison life may be due not so much to a lack of sincerity behind the rhetoric but to naïve adherence to a set of principles which are, in the final analysis, misconceived and unrealistic.

When we examine the prison system as an integral, dynamic component of the general social system and not as an enclosed, discrete subsystem and when we raise our gaze from the individual offender and the reasons and justifications for imprisoning him in a particular criminal case and take into view whole classes of offenders – who might or might not be imprisoned – society's relationship with the penal system takes on an altogether different complexion. From this wider perspective, it is imperative to find correspondingly broader grounds for the justification of the penal system. The common-sense view of the purpose and justification of prison is that it is to control and reduce crime in society. Durkheim and Foucault have questioned this and proposed that the prison fulfils, on the behalf of society, other unspoken purposes that may even run counter to the apparent objective of crime control. The enduring failure of prison to impact on crime and the strong possibility that it actually exacerbates the crime problem and creates criminals or more hardened criminals lends considerable credence to these radical views. No serious critique of the Irish prison system can afford to ignore these provocative analyses that locate the penal system within broader socio-political power structures. Equally, no serious critique can afford to ignore the crucial roles of social justice in crime and punishment and of crime and punishment in social justice.

The questions that need to be addressed, then, are obviously complex, multi-layered and intersecting, involving moral, philosophical, social, psychological and political issues as well as the strictly criminological and penological questions. We must interrogate the prison system not only to see if it works, or works as well as it could, but also to see if it is a just and legitimate enterprise that can be supported by a morally alert community. These questions can, perhaps, usefully be reduced to two inter-related general questions: What functions does society intend prison to serve? and what functions does prison actually serve? In other words, what, on the one hand, are the *intended* effects of prison – on both the prisoner and on society – and what, on the other hand, are the *actual* effects of prison? In the process of examining and elucidating the intended effects in the light of the actual effects, it will obviously be necessary to address the fundamental issue of the role of a penal system in a just society.

2. A sketch of the Irish prison system

Before proceeding with any attempt to answer these complex, far-reaching questions, it is obviously important to obtain a clearer and more detailed picture of the Irish prison system in an effort to discover whether it can be said to work or work as well as it could. It is necessary to describe and analyse the multiplicity of mundane problems that are and will remain critical, whatever understanding one might reach about the deeper purposes and social functions of imprisonment. For this reason, it will be useful to present brief outlines of the Irish prison system and of the nature of the crime problem to which it is a response. This will provide at least a basic factual picture of crime and of the prisons, their regimes and prisoners. These basic facts are essential to any comprehensive understanding of the specifically Irish use of imprisonment.

One fundamental fact is that Irish society and the penal system in particular have experienced enormous and profound change over the last few decades. In 1961, the daily average number of prisoners in the country, including unconvicted remand prisoners, was only 447. In the following three decades, as a consequence of large increases in both the numbers committed to prison and longer prison sentences – in the past few years, most notably for drugs and sex offences – the Irish prison population more than quintupled to stand at over 2,200 in 1991. According to a comparative study,[10] Ireland, among the Council of Europe countries, had by far the most rapid growth in its prison population in the seventeen-year period to 1987. In that time, the number of Irish prison places increased by 156 per cent compared to an increase of only 19.8 per cent in the U.K, a country which suffered even greater increases in crime over the relevant period.

This huge growth in the number of prisoners has not been matched by an equivalent growth in facilities and services or by an appropriate evolution of regimes. Indeed, the current system still, in the main, relies on old Victorian prisons, which are grossly overcrowded, often insanitary and manifestly inadequate to fulfil the functions of a modern penal institution. Many hundreds of Irish prisoners are doubled up in single cells without sanitation. The custom of 'slopping out' of night waste buckets is still a feature of some older prisons. Mountjoy, which opened in 1850 as a penitentiary designed for the 'silent and solitary' system of single-cell occupancy, was meant to house only 440 prisoners. In 1999, more or less the same accommodation in Mountjoy has, on occasion, been used to hold over 800 prisoners and regularly houses 750. No less than three of the present prisons are old Victorian army glasshouses, occupying far-flung, neglected corners of large barracks in Cork, Dublin and the Curragh. These buildings have been refurbished to a reasonable standard but this cannot disguise their total unsuitability. They remain depressing, exceedingly cramped places with little scope for the development of rehabilitative facilities and with only tiny, token outdoor exercise and recreational areas.

There is, however, a considerable range of different types of prison and regime within the Irish system. There are presently fifteen different institutions, including two medium-sized modern prisons with satisfactory facilities, three small open prisons, a training prison with special work and training facilities, a prison for young offenders, an excellent new women's prison, a high -security prison, used to hold disruptive, subversive or political terrorist prisoners, two long-stay prisons, which hold sex offenders and murderers and similar categories, and four older prisons, Limerick, Cork, St Patrick's and Mountjoy, which in fact handle the vast majority of prisoners passing through the system and have by far the worst conditions.

In early 1999, the total number of prisoners stood at about 2,500. However, the number of prisoners is set to increase dramatically, since the government has made a commitment to providing 1,500 extra prison places in the next couple of years. One new prison of 400 places, at Clover Hill, is specifically for remand prisoners and, it is argued, is necessitated by the recent change in the bail laws, which allow for preventative detention of accused people for the first time under modern Irish law. There are quite large prisons newly built or being built at Castlerea and Portlaoise.

Principally, this building programme is an effort to solve the problem of overcrowding and to end the policy of wholesale early release of prisoners, quaintly called 'shedding', which is currently dictated by the lack of prison accommodation. At present many hundreds of prisoners are released early, sometimes very early from their sentence because of prison overcrowding. These prisoners, in effect, serve their sentences at liberty and without meaningful supervision, although they have to sign on at the prison on a regular basis. It is widely agreed that this is a highly undesirable situation not only because it undermines the deterrent value of a prison sentence and brings the criminal justice system into disrepute, but also because it severely affects the morale of the prison system and creates immense difficulties for the planning and organisation of rehabilitative services. The turnover of prisoners, in committal prisons like Mountjoy, is very rapid and a prisoner's length of stay is hardly any longer predictable from his actual sentence length. A number of judges have spoken out about the problem of shedding and pointed out that it undermines their independence and is destructive of the goals of sentencing. Police and victims and their families have also been vociferous about their disgust at finding serious offenders, who had been incarcerated by the courts for quite lengthy periods, out on the streets after a few days or weeks. The widespread practice of shedding clearly makes a mockery of the law and substantially adds to the climate of intimidation and fear of crime in the community. It also greatly increases the amount of unsupervised discretion exercised by the executive over the actual lengths of sentence served and so introduces a very real potential for bias and unfairness into the system.

In the larger Dublin prisons, most notably Mountjoy, the largest and most important committal prison in the country, poor material conditions are aggravated by the fact that many and, in Mountjoy, the majority of prisoners are heroin addicts.[11] Many addicts manage to maintain their addiction in prison and there are credible reports of prisoners using heroin or injecting intravenously for the first time in prison. AIDS or HIV-positive status and hepatitis are common amongst drug-abusing prisoners.[12] Syringes and needles, sometimes of crude home-made manufacture, are known to circulate within the prisons and are a serious risk for the spread of these diseases.

Idleness and long periods of lock-up are also features of these prisons, since there is a chronic lack of work, educational and recreational facilities. In general, even for the prisoners lucky enough to have purposeful occupation in the school or in a workshop, lock-up time averages between seventeen and eighteen hours a day. Prisoners are allowed only one hour of outdoor time per day, which is usually spent in a very constricted, high-walled concrete or tarmacadam yard, lacking the least vestige of natural greenery.

Throughout the system there is a dire shortage of rehabilitative services and limited medical and psychiatric services. There is a substantial educational service, but it manages to impact on only a minority of prisoners. A new sex offender treatment programme is in place but it manages to treat less than 10 per cent of the large group of sex offenders passing through the system. There is a new detoxification centre for the treatment of addict prisoners, but this has only twelve places. One prison of about 100 places has recently been designated as a drug-free prison, but this prison has very little by the way of supportive therapeutic and counselling services and large numbers of inmates are returned to the mainstream prisons from this centre due to failing urine-analysis tests.

There are highly distinctive features of the Irish prison system. For example, the annual cost of holding a person in prison for a year in Ireland is one of the highest in the world. Recent estimates are that an ordinary prison place costs around £50,000 per annum. However, the vast bulk of this inordinate cost is due to the fact that Ireland spends far more money than most other countries on prison officers. This is chiefly because of a very high prison officer to prisoner ratio (1:1 prison officer to prisoner). Most others countries, including many with a reputation for an orderly and humane penal system, manage with a ratio of one prison officer to every three or four prisoners.

Ireland also has, in European terms, a very high proportion of prisoners, who are under twenty-one years of age. About a quarter of Irish prisoners are under twenty-one, while many European countries have less than 10 per cent of their prisoners in this age category.[13] The recidivism rate amongst Irish prisoners is also extraordinarily high by international comparison. A recent survey of Mountjoy prisoners[14] showed that the vast majority (almost 90 per cent) had been in prison before and that, on average, they had been imprisoned following conviction on ten separate occasions.

One of the most significant features of the Irish penal system is the fact that Ireland tends to send to prison a greater proportion of its citizens than any other country in the Council of Europe and about 75 per cent of these have been convicted of non-violent crimes.[15] This is to say, when one focuses on the numbers sent to prison (the imprisonment rate) rather than on the numbers held in prison at any one time (the detention rate), the use of incarceration by the Irish courts is extremely high. Looking at committals under conviction only, we find that the Irish imprisonment rate in 1992 was 174 per 100,000. This compared with only 34 per 100,000 in France, 24 in Italy, 12 in Portugal, and 90 in the Netherlands. These are remarkable differences and demonstrate a comparatively heavy use of the sanction of imprisonment by the Irish courts. The importance of this finding is underlined by the fact that the crime rate is considerably lower in Ireland than in most of the other European countries that use imprisonment far less.

This anomaly has not received the attention it deserves, mainly because the Irish detention rate is quite low by European standards. There are several reasons why the detention rate does not fully reflect the very high imprisonment rate. Most importantly, the current policy of early release, to ease overcrowding, artificially lowers prison population numbers. However, it is also the case that an unusually large proportion of Irish sentences to prison are for very short periods. In particular, about 35 per cent of committals to prison are for failure to pay a fine. Such prisoners, whose offences were originally considered by the court not to merit imprisonment, spend only a short period in prison but obviously extend the resources of the system to an extent disproportionate to their length of stay. The use of short sentences and of the early release mechanism also help explain the very high recidivism rates in Ireland.

Unlike most European countries where the prisons hold a large proportion of immigrants, the Irish prison population is highly homogeneous, with few foreign prisoners, and is characterised by a background of marked socio-economic deprivation, educational failure and lack of vocational training. It is overwhelmingly male and young (under thirty years) with only about eighty women prisoners (3 per cent of the total prison population). In addition many prisoners have alcohol, addiction or psychiatric problems and a large number come from disturbed family backgrounds. In many of the larger prisons, medical, social work and psychiatric services appear to be overwhelmed by the problems they face.

It is important to note that the Northern Ireland 'Troubles' have had a major impact on the development of the prison system in the crucial decades since 1969. In the '70s and early '80s there was a great deal of politically motivated, serious crime within the Republic of Ireland. At one time there were over 200 political prisoners held in the Irish prison system, mainly at Portlaoise Prison. They were often held for grave offences, such as murder, and a substantial number were serving life and forty-year minimum life sentences. Several spectacular escapes and attempted escapes, some involving serious violence or intimidation, led to intensive security wherever these prisoners were held. It would be little exaggeration to state that this aspect of the system received, pehaps quite understandably, a hugely inordinate amount of the administration's attention. The neglect of the mainstream system and the failure to manage the system proactively and creatively in a time of rapid change can in part be put down to the demands on time, thought and resources of the high-security prisons for what the system called 'subversives'.

Some of the key facts about the Irish prison system, then, are:

- The population of prisoners has increased exponentially since the 1960s. Even before the current large-scale, planned increases to a targeted 4,000 prisoners by 2002 got underway, the Irish experience of rapid prison population expansion was unprecedented in Western Europe.

- Until the recent programme of prison building, most of this expansion was catered for by retaining or bringing back into commission old and largely unsuitable Victorian prisons. Only a minority of prisoners are housed in decent modern accommodation with access to appropriate facilities.

- This has inevitably meant that a large number of prisoners live in unpleasant and sometimes inhumane conditions, with poor sanitation including continued use of 'slopping out', and a dire lack of appropriate facilities for work, training, education, rehabilitation, therapy and recreation.

- The continuous increase in prison numbers has been accompanied by chronic overcrowding, especially in the committal prisons and this has had a deleterious effect on regimes and conditions, but it has also led to the widespread practice of early, sometimes very early, release of prisoners (termed 'shedding') because of the pressure on accommodation. This in turn has tended to demoralise the prison system itself and undermine the authority of judges and the faith of the police and the general public in the criminal justice system.

- The Irish courts tend to overuse imprisonment as a sanction in comparison to other Western European countries. Some minor first offenders are imprisoned and many petty-property offenders. About 75 per cent of those sent to prison are sent for non-violent crime. The recidivism rate is extraordinarily high in Ireland partly because so many petty offenders are imprisoned on very short sentences and partly because of the 'shedding' process.

- Compared with other countries, which have systems such as graduated fines and attachment of earnings, Ireland imprisons an extraordinary number of fine-defaulters, that is people who did not pay a court-imposed fine on a conviction that the judge did not consider worthy of imprisonment. Fine-defaulters make up a very small proportion of the prison population at any one time because they serve very short sentences, but they put an unnecessary strain on the system and epitomise the overuse of imprisonment in Ireland.

- Recent figures indicate that about a quarter of those in prison are under twenty-one years. This is totally out of line with the practice in most Western European systems where often as few as 5 per cent of the prison population are this young.

- All the prisons have a drugs problem but the larger Dublin prisons in particular have a serious problem with heroin. Here a majority of prisoners have had a heroin addiction, most frequently involving intravenous use. Many prisoners continue to use in prison and prisons like Mountjoy can be said to be permeated by a hard-drugs culture. Among other problems, this involves the widespread prevalence of disease, most obviously hepatitis. 777, 116 | 365· 09415

• The cost of imprisonment in Ireland is one of the most expensive in the world at over £50,000 per annum per prisoner. Most of this extravagant cost is due to the extraordinary levels of employment of prison officers. There are more prison officers in the system than prisoners. Most other systems have three or four times as many prisoners as prison officers. Despite the generous staffing levels a huge sum is expended annually on overtime pay for prison officers.

3. A sketch of the Irish 'visible' crime problem

If this is a brief profile of most prisoners and of the Irish penal system and how it is deployed, what, then, is the background context of crime in Ireland to which the penal system is society's chief response? The most reliable source of information on the nature and extent of crime is the annual *Crime Report* of the Garda Siochana,[16] but this is by no means an unproblematic source of data. Victimisation studies in Ireland and elsewhere[17], particularly in Britain where they have a regular biennial crime survey, indicate unequivocally that a great deal of crime goes unreported and that a substantial amount of crime in certain categories is reported but goes unrecorded by the police. A rough guide derived from Irish and international studies suggests that there is about three times as much crime as appears in official police statistics. Minor larcenies, public-order offences, vandalism, and petty acts of aggression or bullying constitute most of these unrecorded crimes. Most crime in the more serious categories, such as murder, wounding, aggravated burglary and armed robbery is reported. However, it is certain that there is a further untold number of serious crimes of domestic violence, sexual violence and 'white collar' financial misappropriation that remain hidden and are neither reported nor recorded. These crimes constitute a serious 'invisible' Irish crime problem.

The *Crime Report* gives a statistical accounting of indictable, that is more serious, crime, broken down into: offences against the person, such as murder, rape, and assault; offences against property with violence, such as arson, robbery and burglary; offences against property without violence, such as petty larceny, embezzlement and forgery; and a fourth catch-all category, covering miscellaneous offences such as indecent exposure, misuse of drugs and poaching. The report chronicles, in less detail, non-indictable, summary offences, which normally number about 500,000 in a year. These offences are police defined, in the sense that they are only recorded if a culprit is caught and proceeded against. The majority of summary offences are Traffic Acts Offences, such as speeding, drunken driving and being without insurance. However, the category also covers a large variety of criminal offences such as minor assaults, taking a car for the purpose of joy-riding and public order offences.

In 1947, when the annual Garda report on crime was first published in its current form, crime was at a very low level, about as low as one may imagine crime can be in a modern state. In 1947, there were a total of 15,000 indictable crimes recorded (429 crimes per 100,000 of population). By 1970, this figure had doubled to a total of 30,000 indictable crimes and the following decades have seen an even more rapid increase in crime. The figures for 1983 were more than three times greater than those for 1970. Indeed the increase in indictable crimes in the one year from 1980 to 1981 was greater than the total figure of 15,000 for 1947. In 1995, indictable crime reached an historic peak of 102,000 (2,684 per 100,000 of population), but has declined in both 1996, 1997 and 1998 to now stand at approximately 85,000.

However, even the peak figures for Ireland suggest that it is, comparatively speaking, a low crime country. The Irish crime rate is about half of that for the U.S. (5,060 per 100,000)[18] and a third of that for both England and Wales (9,620 per 100,000).[19] and Denmark, a similarly sized Northern European country (9,960 per 100,000).[20] However, there are inevitably definitional and equivalence problems with such comparisons.

Indictable crime in Ireland is overwhelmingly dominated by property crimes. The largest single category is burglary, which normally accounts for about 30 per cent of all crime. Larcenies of various types account for a further 55 per cent of all indictable crime, with larcenies from unattended vehicles the single largest category in this group (17,000 in 1996). Robbery is also a relatively common crime accounting for about 3 per cent of the total, but armed robbery and armed aggravated burglary are relatively rare, numbering about 550 in 1996.

The most serious crimes are offences against the person and these are also relatively rare. In 1996, there were 1,500 such crimes, but this figure included almost 500 less serious, sometimes purely technical assaults. In 1996 there were forty-six homicides, which is a rate of about 12 per million. This represents a recent increase from a fairly constant average of about 9 per million over the previous twenty years. Thus, the Irish homicide rate is currently at about the same level as that in England and Wales and can be regarded as very low by international norms. By comparison, the Italian rate is close to 30 per million and the US rate is about 98 per million.[21]

One area that has seen dramatic increases in the level of reported crime is that of rape and other serious sex assaults. In the 1980s there were an average of about sixty reports of rape per annum and an average of about 160 other serious sex assaults. In 1996, the figures were 180 for rape and 620 for other serious sex assaults (47 and 166 per million respectively). This marked increase is thought to be mainly due to changing attitudes and a greater willingness to report such crime. However, according to evidence from rape crisis centres, even now, as few as 20 to 30 per cent of rape victims report the crime to the police. The current Irish figures for reported sex crime are, nonetheless, still low by international comparison. For example, in the U.S., there are annually over 400 reported rapes per million of population and in England and Wales over 100 per million.

A very significant development in Irish criminal justice in the last ten years is the exposure of a hitherto unacknowledged level of child sexual abuse by people in positions of trust, such as parents, clergy, sports coaches and care workers. Revelations in this area, often relating to offences dating back several decades, have led to many trials, convictions and long prison sentences. Public, institutional and criminal justice attitudes have been profoundly influenced by these revelations.

While current Irish crime rates are not high by international comparison, the Irish public's perception of the crime problem does not by any means reflect this relatively favourable position. In 1983, American criminologist Freda Adler[22] included Ireland in her study of ten nations around the world with particularly low crime rates. She called this study *Nations not obsessed with crime*. This title now appears ironic since, in recent years, the Irish media and general public have become greatly preoccupied with what they believe to be a severely deteriorating crime situation.

While the fear of crime is somewhat exaggerated in Ireland and has itself become a social problem, there are, nonetheless, a number of reasonable grounds for the intensified public concern about crime. Understandably, Irish attitudes and expectations are shaped mainly by reflection on internal social change rather than by statistical comparison with other countries. In this regard, the last twenty or thirty years have seen a very dramatic decline in the average Irish person's sense of personal security and interpersonal trust, related to the greatly increased crime rate.

The recent exposure of previously hidden crime, such as child sex abuse, rape, and white collar crime, at all levels in society, has certainly had a deleterious effect and fuelled public disquiet. But another major influence has been the role of drug abuse in crime. Heroin and other hard drug use were almost unknown in Ireland before 1979. However, there are now about 13,000 heroin addicts in the socially deprived areas of Dublin[23] and a recent study[24] indicated that heroin addicts are responsible for about two-thirds of all indictable crime in the city.

The advent of serious levels of drug abuse has impacted on the nature of crime in various ways. Individual addicts, who finance their habit through crime, tend to be reckless, desperate and indifferent to victims. This has translated into a growth in the violence of crime and in the breaking of previously well-established taboos against victimising the vulnerable. Old people and women have been targeted to an unprecedented degree, including cases of the torture and murder of old people in isolated rural areas. Another new phenomenon is robbery using a syringe as a weapon. This involves the direct threat of infection with AIDS or hepatitis, which are rife amongst the drug-using population. In 1996 there were 1,100 such robberies in Dublin (and these were, incidentally, at that time not categorised as offences against the person).

The involvement of organised criminal gangs in the importation and distribution of drugs has also had a major negative effect. These gangs have made huge illegal profits and introduced a climate of violence and intimidation new to the Irish crime scene. In June 1996, one such gang organised the murder of the well-known investigative journalist, Veronica Guerin, who was working to expose their operations. There was a huge public outcry at this killing and it led directly to a period of more resolute policing and intense legislative activity. Most of those involved in the killing had been identified and arrested by 1998; however, in the year before Guerin's murder, there were twelve gangland assassinations of criminally involved victims. None of these cases has been solved. An important development in Irish criminal justice has been the shift towards targeting the assets of gang leaders and members. New legislation has empowered the authorities to freeze or confiscate money and property that can be linked to criminal activity and the new Criminal Assets Bureau (CAB) has had considerable success and is credited with breaking up a number of previously almost inviolable drug-dealing gangs.

While the many recent changes in the Irish crime scene do justify public concern, it must also be acknowledged that the small size of the Irish community and its still considerable level of interconnectedness play a powerful role in amplifying the climate of fear about crime. Saturation coverage in the media of gruesome murder cases or ghastly sex crimes resonates throughout Irish society and often provokes an enormous amount of interest and intense emotional reaction in the general public. The fear-mongering tone and selective emphasis of the media on crime issues is undoubtedly influential. The media are centred in Dublin, the one large city, which for many years has had more than 60 per cent of all indictable crime in the country. The understandable focus of the media on Dublin, means that the whole country is very familiar with the situation in the most crime-ridden area and tends to take this situation to be the norm – despite the fact that in some rural areas, such as Co. Mayo, the crime rates are one-sixth or less of the Dublin rates.

Some of the key facts about crime in Ireland, then, are as follows:

- For most of the period from the foundation of the state to the mid-1960s, Ireland was an extremely low-crime country. This was probably linked to the conservative Catholic social milieu, the relatively stagnant, unmodernised state of the mainly agriculture-based economy, and the continuous, large-scale, usually permanent emigration of young people.
- From the mid-'60s rapidly changing social conditions, such as industrialisiation, urbanisation, changes in the family structure and exposure to international media through television, were associated with an increasing level of crime, mainly non-violent property offences. However, also increasing notably were malicious damage, public order offences, car-related crime, such as joy-riding, and some violent offences, such as assault.
- Official figures in Ireland can be questioned and victimisation studies here show that there is a considerable amount of unre-

ported crime and a smaller amount of reported but unrecorded crime. None the less, the Garda Annual Reports on Crime are a useful guide to the incidence of and trends in more serious crime and they indicate that the number of indictable crimes increased from 15,000 in 1947 to 102,000 in 1992. This was an immense increase and it has certainly led to increased public fear of and concern about crime. However, the large differentials in Ireland's favour in comparisons with the crime rates of neighbouring countries have been maintained over this period of growth, since these countries experienced equal or greater levels of increase from their higher base levels. Ireland, therefore remains by comparison a low crime country.

- Recent years have seen a substantial decline in the number of indictable crimes, amounting to a decrease of almost 20 per cent between 1995 and 1999. However, some areas of reported crime have continued to show increases in this period, most notably homicide (the rate of which almost doubled in the early 1990s and has remained high ever since), and sex offences which have shown a sustained year-by-year increase. The increase in sex offences is related to both an increasing willingness to report such crime and, particularly in the area of child sex abuse, to the recent exposure of crimes, which date back many years. The number of armed robberies and burglaries using a firearm has declined dramatically from 582 in 1994 to 221 in 1998. The number of undetected crimes in these two categories has declined from 427 to 133 in the same period.

- The Dublin region currently has about 55 per cent of all the indictable crime in the country. It has a crime rate (42 per 1,000) that is at least twice as high as that of any other Garda region and four times higher than some regions. In general the higher crime rates are found in the more urbanised areas throughout the country. The Dublin region also has the lowest detection rate for indictable crime, but detection rates have been increasing in recent years and now stand at 44 per cent for the country as a whole.

- In the '70s and '80s, many of the most serious crimes in the state were perpetrated by politically motivated groups, such as the Provisional IRA. A great deal of law-enforcement effort was concentrated on this area. There has been a considerable legacy from this period with, for example, ordinary criminals modelling some of their more serious crimes on terrorist group methods, such as kidnapping, and with greater availability and use of firearms.

- The single greatest influence on crime of recent years, however, has been the advent of serious levels of hard drug use (mainly heroin) in Dublin. From 1979, Dublin has had a serious epidemic of drug use mainly amongst the most disadvantaged groups and this has had immense implications for the nature and extent of crime. A recent Garda study has estimated that more than 90 per cent of heroin users commit crime to finance their habit and that two-thirds of indictable crime in Dublin is committed by drug users. This has led to not just an increase in petty property crime but also to new levels of highly lucrative and ruthless organised crime. Desperate drug users can be gratuitously violent even when engaged in minor property theft, but organised crime has introduced serious levels of intimidation and gangland assassination to the Irish crime scene. Since the killing of Veronica Guerin in 1996, new police and legal methods such as the CAB and Operation Dochas have had some impact on both organised crime and street-level drug offences. However, drug importation, distribution and use still continues at high levels and is even beginning to spread to provincial towns. It is important to note that for most of the last two decades the Garda did not target drug use offences *per se* and so official crime figures give little sign of the seriousness of the drug problem.

- In recent years tribunals, scandals and revelations of all sorts have brought attention to the immense amount of hidden crime in Ireland, including sex abuse, domestic violence, and white-collar crimes of corruption and dishonesty. The few thousand white-collar type crimes that appear in the official statistics, however, are mainly the minor crimes, such as social-welfare fraud, of those also convicted for *visible* crime.

4. The links between crime and its punishment

The immediate connection between the phenomenon of crime as defined, recorded and investigated by the police and the world of the prison is, of course, the judicial process of prosecution, trial, conviction and sentencing. At present there is very little statistical information on this central process. Consequently, it is difficult to map the connection between the incidence of crime and the use of the sanction of imprisonment. One major difficulty is that the Garda figures on crime, that is on the 90,000 or so indictable crimes recorded each year, refer to individual incidents, while at the level of the prison we have information only about individual offenders, who may have been convicted for one crime or for dozens of crimes. Furthermore, while there may be around 3,000 people in prison at any one time, in the course of a year, over 12,000 people are sent to prison. Half of these prisoners are on remand and, at present, generally spend only a short time in prison. Around 6,000, however, have been committed under conviction. About 4,000 of these receive a sentence of immediate imprisonment from a judge, while the remaining 2,000 or so undergo imprisonment as the alternative to a fine – that is because they have failed to pay the original sanction of a fine.

It is extraordinary that in 1970, when there were about 35,000 recorded indictable crimes, just under 3,000 people were committed to prison under sentence, whereas in 1980, when there were 72,000 such crimes or more than twice as many, only a couple of hundred more, that is just over 3,000 people, were committed to prison under sentence. This indicates that there is no straightforward, necessary connection between the amount of crime committed or at least recorded by the police and the number being sent to prison. This interpretation is confirmed by the fact that in both the mid-'80s and the mid-'90s, immediately following periods of peak levels of recorded crime, but when recorded crime was actually declining, there were marked upswings in the numbers being committed to prison by the courts. Between 1980 and 1985, there was a 50 per cent increase in the numbers sent to prison and this new higher use of imprisonment was maintained in the late '80s, despite the stabilisation of crime and indeed some notable decreases in crime. Between the years 1990 and 1995, the new, high rate of imprisonment of the 1980s was further built upon, and almost 2,000 more people per annum were sent to prison in 1995 than in 1990.

There are no available, detailed studies providing analysis of these important trends. Nor is there data to clarify the relationship between the use of imprisonment and the extent of recorded crime, the pattern and seriousness of offending, the characteristics of offenders, and the success or otherwise of prosecutions and Garda investigations. However, it appears evident from the available figures that the judiciary, in the '70s, were at that time able to resist resorting to imprisonment, despite huge increases in recorded crime. However, when in the '80s they, for whatever reason, began to resort more frequently to imprisonment, this increased reliance on prison quickly became an ingrained habit that proved very difficult to reverse, even in periods when recorded crime was declining.

The Garda claim to detect a little over 40 per cent of all recorded indictable crime. However, only about one-third of all indictable crime is proceeded against in court. This amounts to about 30,000 crimes. Every year, approximately 18,000 individuals are proceeded against with respect to these 30,000 crimes and we can assume that the 6,000 offenders sentenced to prison are largely from this group, although a number of the imprisoned will have been convicted for non-indictable crimes. Reliable data are lacking on the number of guilty pleas versus contested trials and on the breakdown of trial verdicts in terms of acquittals and convictions. Data are also lacking on the specific use made by the court of alternative sanctions, such as fines, community

sanctions and fully suspended sentences of imprisonment. Ignorance also reigns about the crucial relations between the use of
these various alternative sanctions and both the type of offence
being sanctioned and the characteristics and criminal history of
the offender. However, the Probation and Welfare Service, which
supervises the community sanctions of probation, community
service and supervision during deferment of penalty, provide
figures on the number of offenders, with whom they deal. A little
over 4,000 offenders receive community sanctions each year,
broken down into approximately 1,000 Probation Orders, 1,750
Community Service Orders and 1,250 Supervisions during Deferment of Penalty.

One final component of the complex mosaic of the criminal
justice system is the Juvenile Diversion Scheme. This is a pre-
prosecution diversion scheme for young people under eighteen
years of age. It is run by the Garda Siochana and involves a
formal or informal caution and sometimes the supervised
involvement of the offender in a community-based programme.
This important scheme operates to keep young people out of the
courts. Recent figures indicate that about 15,000 young offenders
are referred annually to the National Juvenile Liaison Office,
which represents a large increase in the use of the scheme over
recent years. About 3,000 young offenders are referred on by the
Office for prosecution in the normal manner, but the remainder,
a very substantial 12,000, are dealt with by cautions and the
other alternative methods and do not gain a criminal record.
Larceny, burglary, criminal damage and vehicle offences account
for well over half of the offences notified.

We can conclude that on an annual basis, at present,
upwards of 10,000 offenders are convicted and receive a sanction other than a fine (which they in fact pay). This latter point is
relevant because a substantial number of those sent to prison
are fine-defaulters, who have been unable or unwilling to pay a
fine. Of these 10,000 offenders, receiving sentences more
serious than a fine, about 40 per cent are sentenced to community sanctions and about 60 per cent are imprisoned. Those sent

to prison overwhelmingly receive short sentences. In 1993, for example, the last year for which there are published statistics, about 2,600 of the 6,000 or so sent to prison were sent for periods of under three months. Well over half were sent for sentences of under six months. Only a little over 500 received sentences of two years or more, and only twenty-five in total received a sentence of ten years or more.

While long sentences are still relatively rare, it must be noted that they have increased considerably over the past few decades. In 1970, there were only thirty sentences of over two years out of the total of about 3,000 sentences handed down, that is about 1 per cent. By 1995 this had increased to 550 sentences over two years out of about 6,000 sentences, that is about 9 per cent. Since people with long sentences accumulate within the prisons, it is obvious that the greatly increased demand on prison places since 1970 is in part due to this very substantial increase in the use of longer sentences. This trend towards longer sentences increases the need for prison places independently of the fact that the overall number of people sentenced to prison has doubled over the same period.

It is instructive to examine the offence type for which people are sentenced to prison. Such an examination tends to dispel the common myths about the nature of the prison population and the use of imprisonment, because it shows that only a small minority of sentenced offenders have committed serious offences against the person. In 1993 only 10 per cent (about 550) of those sentenced to prison were convicted in the most serious category of offences against the person. Six were convicted of murder, fourteen of manslaughter, fifty-eight of wounding, twenty-one of rape and forty-one of indecent assault. However, 400 of the group cannot all be regarded as truly serious, since they received short sentences for the often minor or technical offence of assault. A further 245 offenders were convicted in the category of offences against property with violence – for aggravated burglary, robbery and attempted robbery. However, the vast majority of offenders were convicted for relatively minor offences against property, including almost 2,000 for various kinds of larceny. Strangely, only 150 were convicted for burglary, which is the most common individual crime in the country, according to Garda figures. Astoundingly, 233 people were sent to prison for drunkenness and 281 for debt or contempt of court and just under 1,600 were convicted and imprisoned under the Road Traffic Acts, not including the obviously serious cases of dangerous or drunk-driving.

This admittedly brief and patchy outline of the Irish criminal justice system and the links between crime and punishment clearly conveys the complex and frequently chaotic nature of the system. It is a very common assumption that the purpose of the criminal law and of penal sanctions is the control of crime in society. This is the perspective that underlies our current penal system. Even if one uncritically accepts the validity of this perspective, and I will argue later that it is not in fact tenable, it is obvious from the evidence described here that there are many incoherent, ineffective, unjustifiable and self-defeating aspects of the Irish system. Even if we do not question the social construction of crime in Ireland, including, at the most practical level, the influence of public perceptions, legal and legislative definitions and police discretion, the distance between the commission of crime at one end and the use of prison to sanction criminals at the other is very great indeed.

Many different processes shape the final outcome. One obvious feature of the system is that only a small part of the crime that is committed is recorded, solved and processed through the system to result in the eventual punishment of an offender by imprisonment. Analysis of the British Crime Survey and British police, court and prison statistics[25] has indicated that only 3 out of every 100 crimes against individuals and their property in Britain result in a conviction or police caution. An even smaller proportion of crimes eventuate in imprisonment. Of course, those finally convicted may have committed a considerable proportion of the crimes that are unreported, unrecorded or not cleared up. Nonetheless, this is a stunning statistic with far-reaching implications. While the situation in Ireland may not be as extreme, the general picture holds. Only a small minority of crimes are finally cleared up with the conviction of an offender known to have committed that crime. One dramatic conclusion that can be drawn from this finding is that the person contemplating an offence need have very little anxiety about the possibility of capture or about being held responsible before the criminal law for that particular offence.

This insight into the operation of the system strongly challenges the perception of the penal system as an effective, or even meaningful, deterrent mechanism with respect to people motivated to commit crime. It raises serious misgivings about the supposed crime control purpose of the penal system. It also provokes questions about the composition of the prison population and why the particular people who end up in prison come to be selected for imprisonment – the sanction of last resort and most serious punishment available to Irish society. Not only does much 'white-collar crime', domestic violence and sexual violence escape the attention of the law, but it would appear likely that only a selected proportion of those committing the common-or-garden types of *visible* crime, such as larceny, robbery and burglary, end up in prison.

Social change as the backdrop to an evolving penal system

While a review of the facts of the criminal justice system generates much evidence of this kind, with an important bearing on the deeper questions of the social functions of prison and of its legitimacy, I will for the moment focus on those failures and deficiencies that impact at a practical level and are relevant to the common-sense understanding of the prison as a mechanism for the control and reduction of crime. It will be useful for this critique of the current operation of the Irish prison system to have a comparative dimension, that is to reflect on similarities and differences between Ireland's and other countries' crime and penal problems and their responses to those problems. Equally this critique must be rooted in a contextual understanding of historical developments and of rapidly evolving social change.

For most of this century,[26] probably reflecting the stagnant state of the economy, the high level of emigration of young people and the highly conservative social milieu, crime was not a serious problem in Ireland. However, as I have described, from the mid-'60s onwards there was a phenomenal growth in crime, which was undoubtedly linked to the concurrent profound social and economic changes. The speed and unexpectedness of the growth in crime and the inherent inertia of Irish political and institutional life meant that the criminal law and institutions, like the courts and the prisons, changed very little in structure or outlook in response to the changing circumstances. These institutions tended to be complacent, backward-looking and inflexible and so wholly ill-equipped to deal with the very much greater and more complex demands suddenly placed on them in the last quarter of the twentieth century. Only slowly has Ireland woken up to the fact that the criminal law is not an immutable monolith but can be actively shaped and remodelled as the legislature deems appropriate.

This latter period has witnessed a rapid process of industrialisation and urbanisation and the opening-up of Ireland to the powerful influence of global media, international market forces and the values of consumerism, individualism and materialism. These profound changes have been concentrated into a relatively short time-frame and have, therefore, been particularly intense and disturbing. Ireland is now in the throes of a period of unprecedented economic growth indicated by a boom in building and infrastructural projects, a very significant increase in the numbers at work and transformation into a country with net immigration. Social realities and social structures are metamorphosising before people's eyes but in an unplanned, unpredictable, perhaps indescribable way. The old order of values has been challenged and, indeed, largely dismantled. For example, Ireland has experienced radical change in the organisation of the family, especially with regard to decline in the cohesion of the extended family and to growth in both marital breakdown and single parenthood.[27] The rapid evolution into a developed, affluent, high-technology driven economy has also been accompanied by an abrupt and profound secularisation and intensified social competitiveness, both in the workplace, in the economy generally, and, most crucially, in the education system. The new Irish society, confident in its ability but unsure of its values, is still, however, marked by extremes of poverty and a severe degree of social exclusion of the poor and other minorities[28].

These pervasive changes and the persistent inequalities of Irish society impact in numerous ways on both crime and the use made of the prison system. For example, the heroin epidemic, which has engendered a mass of organised crime and petty individual crimes, has clearly impacted to an enormously disproportionate extent on the disadvantaged sectors of the Dublin population. These people, suffering from poverty, under-education, unemployment and lack of opportunities were both susceptible to the excitement, euphoria, sense of escape, and other attractions of drug use and ill equipped to perceive and resist its dangers. On the other hand, the drugs epidemic can also be clearly related to the globalisation of modern society, to increased accessibility and international travel and even to the creation of a single market within the EU.

Again, the growing affluence of Irish society and the proliferation of consumer goods along with continuing genuine deprivation have led to an enormous growth in acquisitive crime. But increased affluence has also had the effect of raising general expectations about personal comfort and security. For example, our society is increasingly concerned with controlling risks of all kinds, including the risk of criminal harm to persons and property. These attitudinal changes have resulted in the toleration of widespread surveillance of public places by CCTV, but may also be related to growing intolerance of and punitiveness towards petty criminals involved in public order offences and theft.

5. The chaos and multiple deficiencies of the system

While there is little Irish research that analyses the complex interactions between social change and criminal justice phenomena, the relevance of social conditions to crime and punishment is undeniable. This is an era in which even the social meaning of crime and punishment – not just their concrete nature and incidence – is constantly shifting. However, in order to critique the penal system, it is useful to classify the problems of the system into four different categories with respect to: 1) material resources and service provision; 2) internal management of the prison system; 3) social policy and co-ordination problems within the broader criminal justice system; and 4) the political dimension. Across all four categories the response of the prisons administration and their political masters to the challenges of recent decades has been characterised by inaction, lack of adaptation, incompetence and a dire failure of imagination with respect both to understanding the challenges faced and setting realistic targets and standards to be achieved. The standards and targets that have been set have rarely been met and, where there is evidence of improvement, the pace of change is usually glacially slow. The introduction of progressive elements into the penal system has been beset by tokenism, and undermined by a lack of commitment and ambition and by the provision of grossly insufficient resources.

It is obvious from the preceding brief reviews of the prison system and the crime problem that these four problem categories must be examined within the broader social context and are themselves intimately inter-related to such an extent that the failures of the system can only be clearly discerned and fully acknowledged when links are made between all four categories. So, for example, the self-defeating travesty of unprogrammed early release and some of the most appalling material conditions in the prisons are the direct result of overcrowding. But overcrowding is not, as the system appears to perceive it, an unpredictable and unmanageable act of nature. Overcrowding itself is the direct result of lack of planning, the failure of the administration to adopt straightforward, sensible measures, such as waiting-lists for prison, and the social policy failure at the political level to develop enlightened sentencing practices and an adequate system of alternative sanctions to custody. Therefore, while the following analysis breaks down the problems of the system into manageable chunks at four clearly identifiable levels, it strives at the same time to take an integrated analytical approach that takes account of the interconnections between the levels and of the broader social context.

Poor conditions and services

Material conditions are poor in all the old Victorian prisons, but worst in Mountjoy, where it is commonplace for as many as seven newly arrived prisoners to be sleeping on mattresses, or even on tables, in one small room.[29] It is not unusual for two or three prisoners to share a cell, originally intended, in 1850, for one person. On average, prisoners are locked up in their cells for seventeen or eighteen hours per day and often enough for twenty-three hours. For almost half of all prisoners throughout the prison system, slopping out is still the degrading reality. Bodily wastes are deposited into a plastic bucket, which sits in the corner of the cell, waiting to be carried through the prison and emptied into a sluice in a ghastly early-morning, ritual parade. For many prisoners washing, shaving and teeth-cleaning is a hurried routine enacted in a communal washroom adjacent to these sluices. Except in the open prisons, all meals are collected from a trolley or a hatch and eaten in the cell. For most prisoners, showers and a change of clothing are a relatively rare privilege.

Idleness is endemic and only a minority of the prisoners are able to pursue productive activity in the school, the workshops or the kitchens or in the maintenance of the prison itself. Most of this activity, when available, is curtailed by the very short out-of-cell times permitted by the regime, but, paradoxically, prisoners who work in the kitchens are required to opt into twelve- and fourteen-hour working days. Although in the Curragh Prison inmates are provided with televisions in their cells and although Wheatfield Prison has excellent outdoor and indoor exercise areas, this level of provision is exceptional. Exercise and recreational facilities for the vast majority of prisoners are extremely poor or non-existent. Overcrowding and the doubling-up in cells has also led to an apparently new, horrific phenomenon in Irish prisons – sexual assault of prisoner by prisoner. There have, in fact, been two recent court cases relating to the rape of a cellmate by a prisoner.

Worst of all is that prison life for many is dominated by a rampant drugs culture. Almost two thirds of Mountjoy inmates, and large numbers in other prisons, have been heroin users and many of these, perhaps more than half, attempt to continue using heroin in prison, at least on an occasional basis. The mechanics of smuggling and of the concealment of 'works', drugs, and drug use itself preoccupy many prisoners' lives. This can frequently spill over into disputes and quite severe intimidation, even of non-drug-users. These latter are sometimes targets of coercion to become involved in smuggling drugs, because they are perceived to attract less surveillance during visits or on returning to the prison from an excursion to court or elsewhere. Many of the drug-using prisoners are HIV positive and the majority have hepatitis. For many years, before the recent opening of the special Medical Unit, prisoners with advanced illness were quarantined in a prison within a prison in Mountjoy. This was a dark and dismal dungeon of a place, set back from the main building – one of the most ghastly and unhappy places imaginable. It was a sad and scandalously inappropriate setting for sick and, sometimes, dying drug-addict prisoners.

Currently, many drug-abusing prisoners share syringes and thereby put themselves at risk of disease or endanger others. Some naïve young prisoners are persuaded to inject for the first time in prison and foolishly place themselves in double jeopardy. No one in the prison can avoid the nastiness and the dangers of the drugs culture, even those who have no interest in the questionable benefits of drug use – the few moments of excitement, euphoria and escape from the oppressive world of the prison.[30] In a recent survey of about 100 Mountjoy prisoners,[31] two non-drug-using prisoners claimed to have been accidentally pricked by syringe needles hidden in other material. Another claimed to have been pricked in the course of a fight. The extent of the prison drugs problem is now clearly immense. While it is true that the scourge of drugs crept up on the system, growing year by year, it did not creep up surreptitiously. As long ago as 1981, a study[32] provided a detailed picture of the seriousness of the drugs problem in prisons and indicated its huge potential for growth. Until the last few years the official response was inertia, indifference and fatalistic resignation to the harm created by drugs both for prisoners and for the prison system. The new Medical Unit Detoxification Programme is a step in the right direction, but since it deals with only twelve addicts every few months – in a system with perhaps a thousand addicts – it can hardly be judged an adequate response.

The medical, psychiatric and other therapeutic services for drug addicts and for other prisoners are generally woefully inadequate. There are some exceptions and some areas of good practice. Dental care is well-provisioned and some HIV-positive prisoners now receive, under a special scheme, very expensive anti-retroviral medication, just as any other citizen might. However, in Mountjoy, the main medical service is provided by two GPs on contract to the prison. Studies of the prison population and Visiting Committee reports document a constant stream of complaints about this part-time medical service. Most complaints concern the perfunctory and sometimes callous nature of medical care provided for the ordinary prisoner. Infamously, statistics have shown that the Mountjoy doctors would often see as many as sixty prisoners in an hour – an average consultation time of about one a minute. Medical consultations frequently take place in the presence of several prison officers and with a standing prisoner and a seated doctor communicating loudly with each other across the full width of a large room[33].

The Mountjoy Visiting Committee has also been at the forefront in exposing some of the deficiencies of the system in its response to the many psychiatrically ill and emotionally disturbed prisoners. The 1993 report,[34] for example, states that 'there may be as many as 10 inmates in Mountjoy Prison who are psychotically ill and undiagnosed and there are many more who are "situationally ill" and entitled to "therapeutic immunity".' The continued misuse of padded cells to hold mentally ill and suicidal prisoners is a stark symptom of the crisis in the system of care for mentally and emotionally vulnerable prisoners. The 1995 Visiting Committee report[35] quoted Dr Charles Smith, Director of The Central Mental Hospital, which provides the visiting psychiatric service to the Dublin prisons, as saying that psychotically-ill inmates are being placed in padded cells for many days at a time. Another startling symptom of the inadequacy of our system in this area was the provision, in 1994 in the newly refurbished Women's Prison, of no less than three padded cells for an average of less than forty women prisoners. The deliberate, well-planned inclusion of these padded cells in a new, improved prison is a chilling reflection of the low aspirations of the administration for its female prisoners and of its evident willingness to turn to out-moded, inhumane, and degrading methods of control as a matter of first resort.

Another stark reminder of the unacceptably low standards in this area were the events in the Women's Prison during the Mountjoy riot of 1983. At that time a number of women broke into a wooden cupboard in the Chief Prison Officer's office, where a huge candy jar of largactil – a powerful anti-psychotic medicine – was kept. A number of them overdosed on this drug and six women prisoners ended up in hospital intensive-care wards. The women knew of this jar because largactil was frequently doled out, almost like smarties, to disruptive and distressed women prisoners by prison officers acting on no more than a telephone mandate from a doctor.

Eventually acknowledging some of the serious problems in the use of prescribed medication, the prison administration appointed a pharmacist for the prison system in 1992. However, her tenure was short-lived, very probably reflecting her frustration at failing to get the system to introduce the necessary reforms and much-needed pharmaceutical control protocols. The post of pharmacist to the prisons has remained vacant ever since. Equally, the Director of Medical Services, appointed in 1989, amid official protestations about the need and intent to radically reorganise prison medical services, has failed to make a major impact. Indeed, on a *Prime Time* television programme on RTE in April 1999, one of the Mountjoy prison doctors, in the course of a spirited, if eccentric, defence of his prison medical practice, announced that the Director of Medical Services 'was not his boss'. Indicative of the managerial chaos in the system, when asked who was his boss, he replied that it was the governor of the prison – an assertion which the governor himself totally denied. During the interview, this doctor also proclaimed that 'all prisoners are liars' and admitted that he did the job for holiday money and, we were left to assume, for no other reason.

Fifteen years ago, the Whitaker Committee,[36] and, more recently, the European Committee for the Prevention of Torture[37] recommended the setting-up of a small psychiatric clinic within the prison system to be staffed by Health Board personnel. Nothing came of this. The Whitaker Committee also recommended that psychiatrists should have direct clinical responsibility for all prisoners suffering from mental illness, disorders of personality, problems of addiction, and for those prisoners of sub-average intelligence with associated behavioural problems. This would have been a revolutionary step in the treatment of prisoners but again nothing came of it. Shamefully, the same inadequate form of intermittent, visiting psychiatric care exists today as in 1985, only this service is now, given the increased presence in the system of various categories of vulnerable prisoner, so much more obviously just scratching at the surface of need.

One measure of the failure to provide adequate psychiatric and therapeutic services is the growing number of suicides and other deaths in the prisons. Before 1980, suicide was very rare in the Irish prison system, but this situation has been reversed and Ireland now has a considerably higher prison suicide rate than Britain and some other European countries. Between 1990 and 1997 there were twenty-three clear-cut suicides and a further eleven cases of deaths related to drug overdoses. In 1993, a departmental working group made a series of fifty-seven recommendations on suicide prevention,[38] but, according to a recent review of progress,[39] many of the key recommendations that would impact on the mental health climate within the prisons have not been implemented. In 1989, an internal Department of Justice report[40] on the suicide problem recommended that people diagnosed as in a suicidal crisis should never be isolated in padded cells, but rather should be immediately hospitalised. However, the inhumane practice of isolation, in the exceedingly depressing and depersonalising environment of a padded cell, still continues. This report also recommended that prison officers coming upon a prisoner hanging in his cell at night should have the capacity to enter the cell and cut down the prisoner. At that time, in the supposed cause of good security, the officer had to leave the landing to find a superior officer, who could furnish keys to the cell. Again, this totally unacceptable practice, which could on occasion prevent the saving of a life, is still the rule in our prison system.

Essential ancillary and after-care services, required to improve the chances that ex-offenders will return to a more ordered, law-abiding life, are also in a parlous state. Facilities for families to visit prisoners are poor and in general the prisoner's opportunities to communicate with the outside world whether through visits, letters or the telephone are very restricted. This isolation puts additional strain on a prisoner's often already fragile personal relationships. Meanwhile, in the community there is little special support for prisoners' partners and children, who frequently confront uniquely difficult problems of stigma, exclusion and poverty. The concept of through-care, that is the active preparation of prisoners for their release and the provision of assistance to them in the immediate post-release period, is totally under-developed. Newly released prisoners often face, without significant support, many severe practical problems, such as unemployment and even homelessness, and problems of emotional and social adjustment, all of which make a return to a criminal or drug abusing lifestyle more likely.

It can be no surprise, when basic physical, social and psychological conditions in Irish prisons can be so poor, when the general rehabilitative potential of prison is undercut rather than tapped by existing regimes, and when provision in key areas such as medical and psychiatric care is so unsatisfactory and under-developed that more specialised therapeutic services for groups, such as violent offenders and sex offenders, are minimal.

A recent paper by the clinical psychologist,[41] who runs the only therapeutic programme for imprisoned sex offenders, notes that, in November 1998, there were 279 sex offenders in prison with an average sentence of six and a half years. These tended to be serious offenders whose offending was 'characterised by repetition and persistence or the use or threat of violence'. This paper, while acknowledging the barriers to effective therapy in the prison environment, states that it is 'critically important that effective interventions with imprisoned sex offenders, aimed at reducing the risk such men present to the community on their release, form part of any comprehensive social policy committed to the reduction of sexual victimisation.' The paper goes on to say that the Curragh Prison, the main institution catering for sex offenders (ninety-two prisoners), has 'absolutely no therapeutic services available for sex offenders'. In 2000, seventy-eight of the presently imprisoned sex offenders are due for release, but few of them will have benefited from the single therapeutic programme available in Arbour Hill Prison, which can treat less than twenty prisoners per year.

In light of all this evidence, it is hard to disagree with the view that the Irish system not only fails to confront the inherent institutional problems of prison but seriously compounds them. The American Friends Service Committee has eloquently described the kind of problems that almost every prisoner must face:[42] 'the basic evils of imprisonment are that it denies autonomy, degrades dignity, impairs or destroys self-reliance, inculcates authoritarian values, minimizes the likelihood of beneficial interaction with one's peers, fractures family ties, destroys the family's economic stability and prejudices the prisoner's future prospects for any improvement in his economic and social status'. This catalogue of damage that even well-provisioned and well-organised prisons can inflict points to the need for the very prudent use of imprisonment and for substantial efforts to redesign prison regimes so that they are minimally harmful and in some areas, such as education and training for employment, genuinely beneficial. There are pockets within the current Irish prison system where genuinely progressive initiatives are addressing the serious personal problems and deficiencies of prisoners and, in so doing, overcoming some of the disadvantages of the prison setting and some of the detrimental effects of the process of imprisonment on the prisoner.

However, for far too many Irish prisoners the reality of prison life represents a much more extensive list of dangers and disadvantages than those named by the American Friends Service Committee. Yes, the Irish prisons isolate, stigmatise and dehumanise; yes, they disrupt positive relationships and foster unhealthy relationships, but they do much more harm besides. Psychiatrically and emotionally disturbed prisoners and those in an acute suicidal crisis are not guaranteed appropriate treatment but, on the contrary, may be thrust into circumstances that seriously exacerbate their condition. Drug-dependent prisoners are for the most part left alone to deal with their addiction and its consequences. Some previously drug-free prisoners actually become addicts within the prison system. Many prisoners constantly run the risk of exposure to serious diseases, such as AIDS and hepatitis. Many prisoners with an obvious interpersonal problem, in the areas of sexual behaviour or anger management for example, pass through the system without being challenged or without receiving the benefit of the cognitive behavioural therapy programmes that are now known to be of real benefit. So far from developing their personal and social skills, redressing the deficits in literacy and numeracy that are the frequent legacy of a failed educational career, and learning the benefits of a disciplined working routine, the majority of prisoners languish in a nether world of soul-destroying idleness and purposelessness. Of course, it can be argued that prison is not intended to be a benevolent solution to the personal problems of prisoners, but even the least sympathetic members of the public must recognise that a prison system with such poor conditions and rehabilitative services is undesirable and inexcusable because it is very likely to create more crime and more hardened and alienated criminals.

For most prisoners the message of their prison experience, the physical, psychological and social conditions in which they are forced to live, is obvious and stark. They know themselves to be neglected, rejected and, in some minds, totally demonised. Whatever the rhetoric of the courts and the penal system, the concrete conditions they face scream out to them that they have little value as persons or human beings, and that their future holds little hope of improvement. It would not be surprising to find many Irish prisoners, especially those in prison for relatively petty, non-violent property crime, giving their heartfelt agreement to G.B. Shaw's[43] assessment of imprisonment as 'a worse crime than any of those committed by its victims, for no single criminal can be as powerful for evil or as unrestrained in its exercise, as an organized nation'.

Management failures

The internal management of the prison system, in the persons of the Prisons Section of the Department of Justice and Prison Governors, has frequently admitted that it has been running the system in the fire-fighting manner of Red Adair or, that is to say in their own words, they have been involved in a process of 'reactive crisis management'. It is evident that the system has tended, in recent decades, to be overwhelmed by growing numbers of committals and longer sentences and by rapidly changing circumstances, such as the advent of large-scale drug abuse, AIDS and the imprisonment of sex offenders. It is also true that the provision of acceptable, humane material conditions and proper therapeutic and rehabilitative services would be very costly. But it is equally clear that the undoubtedly severe demands on the system, arising in recent decades, and the large expense of a fitting response can never excuse the present, calamitous state of the prison system or fully explain and justify the management failures of the prison administration.

Examination of the record makes it clear that management, down through the years, has been characterised by a laissez-faire, defeatist attitude and by a general failure to confront problems, to plan for them and to act decisively to put solutions in place. The reality of the conditions in Irish prisons, described in the previous section, makes a mockery of the fine sentiments expressed in *The Management of Offenders: a Five Year Plan* and exposes the utter lack of vision and the lack of sincere, proactive commitment to humanitarian values in the management of the prison system. This is not a case of impossible circumstances arriving without warning to overwhelm a well-meaning but beleaguered and impotent administration, but of a clear pattern of mismanagement and management by default that amounts to dereliction of duty through a failure to do what was obviously necessary and definitely possible. To give one more illustration, relating to physical conditions, the Mountjoy Prison Visiting Committee, as far back as 1984, voiced grave and vehement concern over the sanitation facilities, pointing out that 'many of the hot and cold water taps do not operate . . . in some cases the entire toilet areas are continuously flooded. We consider that these conditions are degrading and a disgrace to any community. The situation cannot be excused, more particularly *as it has obtained for years*'.

I have elsewhere documented[44] individual instances of financial mismanagement and scandalous waste of resources, such as the £2 million computer system that never really worked or the £1 million officers' quarters that no prison officer wished to live in. These debacles have usually been caused by lack of planning or by utterly disorganised planning rather than by corruption. But the key point here is that lack of finances cannot credibly or validly be made an excuse for the appalling failures of management to provide decent conditions and services.

Such an argument does not hold water because, for many years, management has committed itself to a deliberate policy of indefensible and grossly wasteful expenditure that dwarfs the amounts lost to hare-brained or ill-conceived schemes. In 1996, it cost an average of £46,000 to keep a person in an Irish prison for a year. This compared with £10,000 in France, £20,000 in Canada and £25,000 in England. These excessive Irish costs are due almost entirely to the astonishingly high ratio of prison officers to prisoners – which stands at more than one officer for each prisoner compared to one officer to between two and four prisoners in most other jurisdictions – and to the massive overtime bill that, incredibly, accompanies this extraordinarily generous complement of prison officer staff. Overtime in 1997 amounted to £29 million and made up 30 per cent of prison service pay, compared with 16 per cent two years earlier.

In 1997, the Prison Service Operating Review Group[45] concluded that 'Irish costs are significantly out of line with those in other jurisdictions' and they drew the unsurprising but damning conclusion that the management of the prisons is 'underdeveloped and ill-equipped to provide a service in the most cost-effective fashion'. With admirable, but in the Irish context quite rare, candour they stated that 'the financial control function within the Irish Prison Service is underdeveloped and no culture of financial responsibility or even awareness appears to exist'.

Of the £100 million yearly current expenditure on prisons, almost 80 per cent goes on pay, the vast majority on prison officer pay. The scandal in allowing this situation to develop and continue is exemplified by two facts. First, the extraordinarily generous provision of staff manifestly fails to impact in a positive way on the regimes and conditions in Irish prisons. One example of this is the situation in the relatively new and well-designed Wheatfield Prison. Here, accommodation for prisoners was organised in units of fourteen cells, each with their own dining and social area. However, the dining areas have never been brought into commission and prisoners still eat alone in their cells as in Mountjoy. Believe it or not, the declared reason for this failure is lack of staff! Another example is that in England with far less staff than the Irish system, they are able to provide prisoners with an average of three hours more out of cell time per day.

Second, it is clear that the overtime bill alone for the last fifteen years, if management had been able to divert it to more useful ends, would have provided sufficient funding to completely replace the out-moded and unsuitable Victorian prisons and replace them with properly designed modern accommodation. The prison officer overtime bill for one year would pay for a decent modern prison for a couple of hundred prisoners. In terms of current rather than capital expenditure, it is also obvious that this money could be far more usefully applied to providing adequate medical, therapeutic and rehabilitative services on an on-going basis.

The scandal is that Irish prisons, even with two or more times the number of prison officers, are unable to provide the level and quality of prison-officer related services that are the norm in most other less generously staffed prison systems. This is a damning reflection on the efficiency of the Irish system and the effectiveness of its management.

The failure to adequately control and structure financial expenditure is clearly at the heart of the management malaise and directly linked to the intolerably poor conditions and services in many Irish prisons. In large part, this is a symptom of the inability of management to strike a correct balance of power with the POA, the prison officers' union. The POA appear to have succeeded in turning the prisons into institutions that exist primarily for the benefit and convenience of their members. This is at one level obviously a question of over-staffing and a ridiculous amount of overtime payment, but it is also a matter of an utter failure by the administration to evaluate the performance of prison officers and seek value for money from them.

The Council of Europe Committee for the Prevention of Torture in their report[46] on their second visit to Irish places of detention drew attention to the ludicrous situation, whereby the endeavour to train staff on in-service programmes, in interpersonal communication skills for example, was seriously hampered by the roster system for scheduling work, negotiated by the prisons' management. This roster system meant that all in-service training had overtime implications and was therefore enormously difficult to arrange and disproportionately expensive to provide.

The failure to confront the prison officers' trade union and insist on proper standards of work and conduct also extends to the key area of discipline. The central administration's cowed approach to the POA has at times tended to undermine the powers of prison governors to control their staff and their prisons. Prison governors themselves have warned[47] of

> the absolute control held by the POA over the effective and efficient management of the Irish prison service . . . almost every single operational decision is influenced by either political considerations or trade union interests and usually to the detriment of good management practice.

One example of this intolerable situation was the case in Limerick Prison where, following representations to head office from the POA, the governor found himself prevented from disciplining officers for ill-treatment of prisoners. He later said[48] that as a result of this inaction 'a "hard core" of basic grade officers who had resorted to ill-treatment of prisoners, had come to feel that they were invincible and immune to any instruction from management'. If the financial failures of management are serious, this kind of failure to exercise proper management control is absolutely critical because it strikes at the very capacity of the prisons to maintain a humanitarian ethos.

These far-reaching problems in the areas of financial management, planning and industrial relations are a severe indictment of the prisons administration. But to understand these serious management failures it is necessary to appreciate the role of the deleterious lack of interest and investment in systems for the provision of data and informed analysis on the penal system that has characterised the management approach for many years. It is also necessary to appreciate the role of the administration's profound and largely unchallenged disregard for its accountability to the general public. The authorities have apparently felt that they can function satisfactorily without ever attempting to obtain an adequate understanding of what is going on in the penal system they administer. The last annual report on prisons to appear was for the year 1994. This report, though suffering from severe limitations, is the most important source of statistical and other information on our penal system, not just for the public but for the Department of Justice itself. There is no way that the department or anyone else can arrive at an accurate understanding of the system, such that can benefit decision-making and policy-making, when the basic bookkeeping on its operation is either not done or is delayed for inordinate lengths of time.

This scandalous failure to publish a statutorily required report is symptomatic of a political and bureaucratic disdain both for the facts and for democratic accountability. It demonstrates a preference for secrecy and a desire to avoid being governed by information and well-argued, factually based analysis. The fact that the public is still being assured about the appointment, at some indeterminate future date, of an independent inspector of prisons – an appointment which was strongly recommended by the Whitaker Committee as far back as 1985 – further highlights the official distaste for effective structures of accountability. The far more complex bureaucracy of the Criminal Assets Bureau was set up in a matter of weeks.

The fact that journalists have had to take the Department of Justice to court to obtain access to reports of the Mountjoy Visiting Committee, which by law should be publicly available, is also compelling testimony to the culture of secrecy and non-accountability. It is, of course, highly germane that the Mountjoy Committee is one of the few visiting committees to take their role as public watchdog seriously, in the process frankly and trenchantly criticising the condition and the management of the prison[49].

The failure to create an accurate and reliable statistical data-base and the almost total lack of investment in research until 1998, when a small research fund was made available, are indicative of an immense, official complacency and, it would appear, a fundamental indifference on the part of those in power to creating the preconditions for real progress and improvement. The failure to even attempt to obtain a systematic, reasoned and empirically grounded understanding of the criminal justice and penal systems has in turn inevitably contributed greatly to the system's lack of fiscal, political, and democratic accountability. The administration's approach is inexplicable unless one accepts the cynical view that politicians and powerful civil service office-holders have actually preferred to operate in an intellectually confused climate, which cloaks criminal justice and penal matters in an obscurantist miasma. The obvious advantage of this double veil of ignorance and secrecy is that it permits greater freedom of action, or indeed neglect and inaction, and provides ready excuses for the evasion of personal, institutional and political accountability.

Lack of co-ordination within the system and lack of coherence in social policy

The criminal justice and penal system is highly intricate, in many ways archaic, and inevitably beset by a substantial degree of fragmentation. However, the police, the courts and the prison system are intimately inter-related and interdependent and must work together within the framework of the criminal law as laid down by common law tradition and by the legislature through statute. Notwithstanding this interdependence, the alarming fact is that the various branches of the system often operate without reference to or understanding of each other, as if they were entirely separate and autonomous. The area of official statistics is just one obvious example of the lack of cohesion and co-operation between the branches of the system. The police and the prisons do not even use the same classification of offences. The court system has barely kept a statistical record at all. However, the lack of co-ordination and mutual understanding spreads far beyond record-keeping into very significant areas of theory and practice that impact on the essential nature and effectiveness of the system.

From the perspective of current social policy about the use of imprisonment there are a number of key issues. There is the continued use of short and very short sentences of imprison-ment. There is the continued use of imprisonment for totally inappropriate categories of offender, such as debtors, fine-defaulters, drunks, the vagrant, petty-property offenders and minor delinquents. There is the continued large-scale use of imprisonment as a sanction for juvenile offenders, sometimes as young as fifteen. There is the continued travesty of unpro-grammed early release, purely on the grounds of overcrowding. And most significantly, there is the scandalous neglect of the development of alternatives to custody – the only approach that offers a solution to the system's deep-rooted problem of overuse of imprisonment and the linked disasters of overcrowding and the 'revolving door' prison.

I have made the point that Ireland uses imprisonment as a punishment more freely than almost all other Western European countries. This is in a context of a relatively low and contained crime problem, especially compared with neighbouring countries. This is a crucially important fact and the failure of the system to acknowledge it and respond to it underlies the incompetence and ineffectiveness of social policy in this area. Of course, it must be borne in mind that the lack of a reliable and comprehensive database on the operation of the system obscures these matters and contributes greatly to Ireland's enduring culture of ineffectual criminal justice and penal policy-making.

International comparisons in the criminal justice area are notoriously difficult. They are riddled with problems of definition and equivalence. The operational and cultural realities of various jurisdictions are also surprisingly variable and by careful selection of examples it is possible to support almost any proposition. For example, Ireland with currently about 3,000 prisoners has a comparatively moderate detention rate. Lithuania and New Zealand, both with almost exactly the same population as Ireland, have about 14,000 and 5,000 prisoners, respectively. Surely, this is evidence that Ireland is quite sparing in its use of prison? However, apart from the question of their greater crime rates, these countries should not be taken as appropriate models since, like the USA. (which detains 1.7 million prisoners, equivalent to more than ten times the Irish detention rate), they are totally out of line with normal practice in advanced Western industrial states. Furthermore, the Irish detention rate is kept low because of shedding and numerous, exceedingly short sentences and, for the moment until the new bail laws kick in, a low proportion of remand prisoners.

Ireland, in fact, is at the high end of Western European countries in its use of prison as a sanction. Ireland tends to imprison a larger proportion of its citizens every year than other countries. Most importantly, these people are, to a very considerable degree, imprisoned for offences which would not attract a sentence of imprisonment elsewhere. They are petty, non-violent offenders – though often, admittedly, highly persistent offenders and often people with drugs problems – who are ideal candidates for community-based, non-custodial or intermediate sanctions, involving some form of therapy.

The principal lesson to be learnt from the experience of other countries is that the use of imprisonment as a sanction is not an immutable process of nature nor an uncontrollable product of social organisation. A society's use of prison can be judiciously manipulated and made subject to deliberate, rational policy-making. In the decades following World War II, Holland experienced a five-fold increase in crime, but, through the implementation of new policies on punishment, reduced its prison population by half.[50] Finland reduced its detention rate from close to 200 per 100,000 in 1960 to 62 per 100,000 today, the lowest in Scandinavia.[51] Austria over the last three decades, in spite of increasing crime, has managed to reduce its prison population.[52] In Germany, in the '70s and '80s, the public prosecutors and judiciary, rather than the legislature, led a revolution in penal policy which saw large reductions in the use of imprisonment and huge expansion of alternative community-based and restorative justice type sanctions. When Germany was reunified, the former East Germany very rapidly reduced its prison population to a fifth of the total that pertained under the communist regime.[53] As Nils Christie[54] has remarked 'it is such erroneous reasoning to look at prison figures and at the penal apparatus of a state as something that has to happen inevitably, as if we were victims of a development that we cannot influence.'

There are four essential aspects to social policy control of the use of imprisonment: 1) practical management systems; 2) sentencing practice; 3) legislation; and 4) an effective system of alternatives to custody. Irish social policy has failed dismally at all four. This failure has determined the present counter-productive use of prison as a sanction in minor cases and, consequently, has contributed greatly to the kind of overcrowding and chaos in the prison system that underpins so many of the other major problems I have already described.

The first of these four aspects concerns simple, practical mechanisms and protocols for managing the use of imprisonment and most importantly for ensuring that people sentenced to a fine will pay off this fine and not end up in prison. It is ludicrous that the sanction of last resort is used so frequently in Ireland for offenders, who, according to the sentencing judge, did not deserve imprisonment. In 1993, 35 per cent of all Irish committals to prison under sentence were fine defaulters. In stark contrast the equivalent figures for Holland and Germany were about 3 per cent and 6 per cent respectively.[55] Other countries have put in place systems which both equate a fine to the individual's ability to pay and maximise the likelihood of a fine being paid, for example, by phasing payments in manageable portions and by attaching earnings. Some countries also ensure that a series of other community-based sanctions come into play for fine-defaulters before resort is made to the ultimate sanction of imprisonment.

The introduction of a waiting-list for prison is another straightforward mechanism – used effectively in many other countries – which has been inexplicably ignored by Irish policy-makers. The main benefits of a waiting-list system are, first, that it enables the system to set legal limits on the numbers allowed in prisons and so prevent the worse excesses of overcrowding and, second, that holding a person on a waiting-list for prison in itself creates an incentive for the offender to behave in a law-abiding manner and affords him or her the opportunity to organise the payment of a fine and so avoid imprisonment.

Other important innovations that have been barely considered in Ireland, but have been introduced successfully elsewhere for recalcitrant, minor, non-dangerous offenders, include imprisonment at weekends only or in the evenings and at night only. These forms of intermediate imprisonment, relying on hostel type accommodation, require minimal security and expenditure and have the immense benefit of permitting offenders to continue with employment and maintain their contact with families and mainstream society, while suffering deprivation of liberty as nearly as possible as the sole punishment.

The second aspect of controlling the use of imprisonment is sentencing practice. In Ireland, a well-ordered, just and coherent system of sentencing is conspicuously missing. There are immense disparities in sentencing from judge to judge, from area to area, and even from case to case within a single judge's exercise of power. As former Supreme Court Judge Hugh O'Flaherty has recently written:[56] 'many years of relatively unfettered discretion for Irish judges has not resulted in an identifiable uniform approach to sentencing.'

Judges often make a studious effort to weigh up aggravating and mitigating factors and calculate fitting sentences according to a theoretical tariff of escalating punishment for increasingly serious crime. However, while it is possible, indeed quite customary, for judges to cite the precedent of earlier sentences in similar cases or relevant appeal court judgements on appropriate sentence length and act as if there were a notional set of normative sentences known to all judges, the discretionary powers of judges are very wide and are regularly used to their full extent. This leads to extraordinary variations in sentences across offences and offenders that are on the face of it very similar. For example, the difference for an offence such as rape can be as wide as between a suspended sentence of two or three years and a twenty-year sentence. Variations from the notional tariff are in fact so wide and so frequent as to render the idea of the tariff merely a judicial myth.

Exemplary sentences, which make a scapegoat of one particular unfortunate offender, for the sake of signalling strong judicial disapproval of particular types of offence, are by no means rare. A recent study by Bacik et al.[57] has even found evidence that the social background of the offender can have a profound influence. It appears that judges are more likely to imprison a person from a deprived area than one from a middle-class area – for a comparable level of crime.

The greatest problem is the familiar one of a lack of an adequate database. We have little or no information on the sentences handed down by the courts. Consequently, there is no tradition of Irish studies on the effects of different sentences on the subsequent conduct of offenders. This condemns the practice of sentencing to an essentially *ad hoc* arbitrariness. The lack of a solid, accessible framework of cumulative, statistical data on past sentencing and on the outcomes of sentences deprives judges of the most useful possible tool for the rational guidance of sentencing.

It also leaves the supposedly independent and impartial judiciary vulnerable to the kind of populism that afflicts Irish political life. It leaves them free to be influenced by, and to reflect in their sentences, the not infrequent media-generated moral panics and popular displays of outrage over certain crimes or types of crime. All this has translated into a situation where Irish courts are excessively punitive in their inclination both to use prison in very trivial cases and to impose very long sentences for some categories of offence. It is partly the dearth of data and analysis and the consequent incapacity of judges to reflect on and evaluate their activities that has allowed Irish sentencing to get totally out of step with sentencing practice in other Western nations. A compelling example of this trend is provided by the evidence that the Irish courts hand down sentences for sex offences that are on average twice as long as those imposed in other Western European jurisdictions.[58]

The class composition of the judiciary may also have a bearing on the excessive Irish use of imprisonment against certain sectors of society and its under-use against other sectors. The legal profession is overwhelmingly middle class and people with first-hand knowledge of life amongst the poor and disadvantaged are extremely rare, if not unknown, amongst the judiciary. Third-level education and an extended period of professional apprenticeship with limited earning power are necessary for the person aspiring to become a lawyer. Yet in 1999, students from a low income or poor background constituted only 1 per cent of admissions to Trinity College, Dublin.[59] This means that the judiciary are in effect a self-perpetuating social elite, who sit in judgement in the criminal courts mainly on the people from the remote far end of the social spectrum. In Britain, the magistracy allows the criminal justice system to involve a wide variety of socially responsive and aware citizens, who are not legally qualified, in the sentencing process, especially in the area of youth crime and petty offending. Such a system is sorely lacking in Ireland, where society's sanctioning powers are concentrated in the hands of a profession that takes very little interest in the criminal law and is, by and large, preoccupied with more lucrative areas of law associated with commerce.

With very few exceptions, Irish judges do not try to broaden their knowledge and understanding of the social or penal predicament of the people they deal with in the criminal courts. This is most obvious in their failure to visit prisons to gain first-hand knowledge of the effects of their sentencing practices. In some countries, such as Austria, judges are legally obliged to visit the prisons on a weekly basis and are even required, on these visits, to sample the food available to prisoners. The ossified social structure of Irish society and the continuing lack of engagement of the judiciary with the reality of their practice undoubtedly impact on the criminal justice system and foster the inflexible, unreflective, arbitrary and over-punitive sentencing that shapes the current penal system.

The third aspect of controlling the use of imprisonment concerns the central role of the legislature in sentencing. The Oireachtas lays down by statute the legally applicable sanctions for various categories of offences. However, parliament has signally failed to take the Irish overuse of prison seriously and has not even begun to construct an effective legislative framework for a balanced, rational, consistent system of sentencing. On the contrary, recent legislative activity has focused on *ad hoc* interference with the system to render it both more punitive and more incoherent. Maximum sentences have been increased in a number of areas, most notably for serious sex offences and drug dealing. The maximum sentences have been increased to life. Mandatory sentences have also been introduced – specifically a minimum sentence of ten years for drug-dealing involving drugs with a street value of £10,000 or more. A new power has also been introduced for the state to appeal the *leniency* of a sentence. All of these changes are intended to, and undoubtedly do, send a message to the judiciary that they are expected to get tougher in their sentencing practice.

Finally, the fourth aspect of controlling the use of imprisonment concerns the introduction and proper resourcing of alternative sanctions to custody. The Irish state has a basic framework of alternatives in place, particularly probation and community service, but there has been a dearth of innovation in this area and, generally, the system is grossly understaffed and under-resourced. Less than 200 probation officers, with huge caseloads, struggle to maintain the system of community-based sanctions in a country that has more than ten times this many prison officers. A 1998 Working Group on the Probation and Welfare Service published an interim report[60] recommending the immediate recruitment of seventy-five new officers – they were needed simply to keep up with the current workload. However, despite huge expenditure elsewhere in the penal system, it required a work to rule by probation officers, in April 1999, to achieve partial implementation of this modest recommendation.

There can be no doubt that in the '70s, in Ireland, there was a major shift to the use of alternative, non-custodial sentences by the courts. Between 1973 and 1983 there was a growth in the use of probation orders from 200 per annum to 1,400 per annum. However, this type of growth was not sustained, even after the introduction of Community Service Orders in 1984. Nor did the shift to community-based sanctions ever cut deep enough or broad enough to achieve the new kind of balance between custodial and non-custodial sentences and the new more liberal calibration of sanctions to offences, which are typical of progressive, Western European nations.

In England and Wales in 1994,[61] only 17 per cent of offenders sentenced for indictable offences received a sentence of immediate custody. By comparison, 31 per cent received a fine and 28 per cent a community-based sanction. There are few reliable statistics on the Irish situation but a reasonable estimate is that, despite far lower crime rates than in England and Wales, offenders sentenced for indictable offences are more than twice as likely to receive a custodial sentence and considerably less likely to receive a fine or community-based sanction.

Of course, this is a controversial area and some analysts, like the conservative polemicist Charles Murray,[62] have argued that crime has been increasing, over the last few decades, in large part because of a much reduced risk of imprisonment for a wide variety of offences. The statistical evidence does indeed indicate that imprisonment was a more frequent response in the past when the actual level of offending was much lower. Murray argues that 'deterrence fails only because the odds of being caught and imprisoned are not high enough, or because the sentence is not harsh enough'. This statement smacks of the unanswerable logic of the Koranic Law, which allows for the amputation of a thief's hand and later the amputation of his other hand, if the original punishment fails to deter.

This line of reasoning fails to appreciate the profound transformation in the definition and understanding of both crime and punishment, which has occurred within modern societies. General public sensibilities, certainly in the developed Western nations, have changed dramatically and it is no longer acceptable, as it was two hundred years ago, for criminal justice systems to inflict whatever level of punishment or brutal pain thought necessary to bring deviant behaviour under control. Criminal justice systems today have to work within the law and within the limits of modern sensitivities about the deliberate infliction of physical and mental pain. Punishments have to be proportionate, just and humane and through the UN Charter on Human Rights there is now an international prohibition on torture and on cruel and unusual treatment of wrong-doers. It is no longer acceptable, at least in Western nations, to 'hang a thief for stealing a sheep, let alone a lamb', even if such a policy is a clearly effective way to end an individual criminal's career and to set a powerful deterrent example for others.

History and the experience of countries such as China that currrently rely on draconian forms of punishment teach us that even totally disproportionate and harsh responses to crime fail to abolish crime. Murray's hardline argument fails to appreciate that the proportion of crime detected by law-enforcement agencies and prosecuted through the courts is so small that the potential deterrent effects of imprisonment on the general pattern of offending are likely to be negligible. Indeed, Tarling[63] has estimated that the prison population would have to be increased by 25 per cent in order to reduce the number of offences being committed by just 1 per cent. In light of this information, we must surely concur with Montesquieu[64] when he states: 'Mankind must not be governed with too much severity . . . If we inquire into the cause of all human corruptions, we shall find that they proceed from the impunity of criminals, and not from the moderation of punishments.'

Murray's 'get even tougher' deterrent approach also ignores the crucial fact that the most rigorous evaluation research available[65] indicates that community-based sanctions are generally every bit as effective as, and often more effective than, imprisonment at deterring petty criminals. These alternative methods also, crucially, avoid the powerful criminogenic effects of imprisonment. These less damaging, less expensive and often more successful approaches are, therefore, to be greatly preferred, when there is no pressing need to lock up an offender because he or she represents a real, live danger to the public.

The restorative justice approach has also been neglected in this country, despite proving its value over many years in countries such as Germany, New Zealand and the USA. Restorative initiatives, such as family-group conferences, are concerned to make the offender take personal responsibility for his behaviour more than with merely punishing him. They also emphasise the needs of the victim and of the wider community and engage both victim and community in the restorative process. This approach promises much because it addresses issues such as reparation, forgiveness and reintegration of the offender in a manner that takes account of not only what the offender must do for the victim and the community but also what the community can and should do for the offender in order to copper-fasten his more constructive behaviour.

The restorative approach is, in a sense, a harking back to an era of more cohesive, intimate and involved communities that were naturally empowered to deal effectively with offenders without severing the positive bonds, as prison does, between the offender and the rest of the community. Restorative justice, therefore, promises much not only in the area of new, potentially more effective techniques and models for dealing with offenders but also in the area of creative new social structures that will build communal bonds as a counterbalance to the growing fragmentation, competitiveness and preoccupation with selfish individualism now prevailing in society.

The failure of policy-makers and decision-makers in all four of the aspects of the controlled use of imprisonment, the failure of the state to co-ordinate its thinking and action in this area, and the even more basic political failure to recognise and address the serious problem of what is a fitting punishment are inexcusable because these omissions have made key contributions to the chaos, inefficacy and poor conditions of the prison system and because they have led, possibly by default but perhaps at some covert level purposefully, to a society that is disproportionately and counterproductively harsh and punitive.

Interestingly, a study by criminologists, Wilkins and Pease[66] has indicated that the extremity of the scale of punishment utilised by a society is linked to its tolerance of inequality: 'countries that have a highly individualistic and competitive ethos, premised on notions of meritocracy and equal opportunity, and have substantial gaps between rich and poor are likely to be comparatively severe in their penal outlook'. This is relevant to Ireland because a recent UN study[67] has shown that, next to the USA., Ireland has the most unequal distribution of wealth of all the developed industrialised nations. Ireland is an increasingly competitive and meritocratic society that unfortunately continues to subject a large minority of its citizens to relatively severe levels of poverty and to very confined opportunities to gain a more substantial stake in society. As we have seen, in line with Wilkins and Pease's predictions, this very socially divided Ireland resorts to imprisonment more readily than most other countries and continues to impose harsh custodial punishment on even trivial offenders.

The political dimension

The political dimension is, of course, pervasive across all of the problem areas I have described. A succession of governments, Ministers for Justice and parliaments have presided over the shameful shambles of the penal system. It is worth noting at this point that, as Tomlinson[68] states, 'the broader political relations between Britain and the Republic of Ireland over the North and the presence of political prisoners in the South itself, have had their effects on the sluggish pace of penal reform and the modernisation of the prison system.' However, the final responsibility for the lack of vision behind the system, for the lack of thought and co-ordinated action, for the appallingly poor conditions and services, and even for the short-comings of prisons management must lie with these politicians. They have the power to reform where reform is obviously necessary and they have the duty to set the goals, priorities and standards necessary for a just, humane and effective penal system. Instead of energetically addressing the multiple problems of the system, the political masters chose, for the most part, to ignore them. However, when the occasion demanded it, they chose to join with the civil service bureaucracy in defensively and wrongly characterising the problems of the system as overwhelming, unmanageable acts of nature or of the social order – problems that were not amenable to their powers and were suited only to reactive crisis management.

By and large, the legislators, even in their more active recent years, have been content to tinker with the system in a piecemeal fashion that has been driven not by the crying need for fundamental reform but by media-created moral panics. The general thrust of legislative change has been towards ever more repression with the introduction of longer maximum sentences and mandatory sentences and new laws that strengthen the powers of the Gardai and limit the rights of suspects and defendants.[69] Some innovations, like the Criminal Assets Bureau and other mechanisms to tackle organised criminals through their finances, are sensible and efficacious, but, in general terms, the change process has been focused on a phoney war on crime and informed by a reactionary 'law and order' ideology and by an imported, hopelessly muddled philosophy of 'zero tolerance'.

The political indifference to the penal system has, on the other hand, not been total. At one point the Department of Justice had to employ an Assistant Principal Officer and six clerks at the work of processing representations from TDs about punishments handed down to their constituents by the courts. Many of these representations were successful and achieved the commutation of fines or even of sentences of imprisonment. This extraordinary example of political clientilism continues today despite the severe criticism of the system by the High Court in the case of Judge Brennan versus the Minister for Justice. The High Court stated that this form of political interference with judicial sentencing is tantamount to a parallel system of justice. Also highly questionable is the practice whereby several Ministers for Justice have decreed that no prisoner from their own constituency will benefit from the early release programme or shedding. For many years the same intrinsically unfair strictures have also applied to all sex offenders. Although this is, perhaps, an understandably popular policy, it demonstrates a culture of interference with and politicisation of the penal system. In the case of sex offenders, it has the additional disadvantage of preventing forms of supervised early release that are considered, by experts in the field, invaluable to the rehabilitative treatment of sex offenders.

The political failure with regard to the penal system is all the more inexcusable because, since 1985, governments and parliamentarians have had access to a lucid, cogent and well-evidenced report that identified most of the problems at the centre of the penal crisis and that recommended the main steps that needed to be taken to improve matters. The *Report of the Committee of Inquiry into the Penal System*,[70] known colloquially as the Whitaker Report, was a very fine, comprehensive analysis of the system that provided many practical and realistic solutions, but was destined to be recklessly ignored by the establishment.

The Whitaker Report identified the core problem of the overuse of imprisonment and recommended principles which would in effect 'reserve imprisonment for serious offences against the person and major property offences'. It recommended a large extension of non-custodial penalties including probation, community service and fines but required that the serious defects in these systems, such as the under-staffing of the Probation Service and the updating of the scale of fines and the provision of a sensible system for their collection, first be put right. Some of the report's recommendations were innovative, including confiscation of income and assets, restitution both to the victim and society, requirement of attendance at treatment centres for alcohol or drug abuse as an alternative to imprisonment and compulsory residence in approved hostels or compulsory participation in training programmes.

While there can be no doubt that the Whitaker Report was shamefully neglected for many years, a case can be made that the long history of political failure to tackle the problems of the penal system is now a thing of the past. In the last few years, there have been major developments and a seeming transformation in the bureaucratic and political culture with respect to the penal system. In the first place, a huge prison-building programme has been undertaken to address the twin problems of overcrowding and the 'revolving prison door'. Large new prisons at Castlerea, Portloaise and Clover Hill and extensions to the present prison plant promise an additional 1,500 prison places in the next few years. At last, a modern, well-appointed women's prison has been built. This expansion, especially the provision at Clover Hill of a prison exclusively for remand prisoners, can be expected to have a major impact on the poor conditions and disorderliness of committal prisons like Mountjoy, which, up till now, have struggled to handle the transient population of remands along with their swelling numbers of convicted prisoners.

Furthermore, an interim, independent prisons board has been set up and a Director of Prisons has been appointed to run the system separately from the Department of Justice. The appointment of an independent inspector of prisons is expected shortly. Drugs courts, which will divert drug-abusing offenders from prison to treatment programmes, are about to begin operation.[71] At least within the juvenile justice area, there is considerable eagerness to experiment with new non-custodial and preventative approaches. The new Childrens Bill will introduce family-group conferencing, a form of out-of-court settlement that will bring offenders, parents, victims, the police and welfare authorities together in an attempt to both hold a juvenile offender responsible for wrong-doing and identify his or her problems and viable means to address them. The new bill will also put the juvenile liaison diversion scheme on a statutory basis and provide for day-attendance orders that compel young people to attend training, educational and activity centres for courses tailored to their needs. Even within the prisons, recent years have seen the introduction of small-scale but highly professional programmes for drug abusers and sex offenders and there are promises to expand these services. The EU-funded Integra programme[72] has also brought a new level of optimism, professionalism and realism to the areas of vocational training of prisoners and their preparation for employment.

Alongside these obviously very positive developments, there has been the gradual emergence of a new, more transparent and open attitude within the Department of Justice. Research reports and other honest appraisals of the system are now no longer automatically suppressed. There has been a National Crime Forum[73] and a White Paper on criminal justice and permanent Crime Council are promised. The Department of Justice, Equality, and Law Reform has itself published an informative and thoughtful overview,[74] entitled *Tackling Crime*, and is now committed to producing a three-yearly strategy plan,[75] laying out its specific objectives. The Minister for Justice has even proposed reducing the prison officers' overtime bill by 40 per cent.

Given this impressive degree of positive change, one might reasonably ask: can anything more be expected? Superficially at least, the right rhetoric and strategies and some of the right structures seem to be in place. However, while there has been a transformation in the system's self-presentation, leading to some minor public-relations triumphs, one does not have to be an implacable cynic to question the genuineness and the actual import of all this apparent change.

The genesis of many of the reforms is especially revealing. For example, the independent prisons board, a long-resisted recommendation of the Whitaker Report, was hurriedly agreed to by Minister for Justice, Nora Owen, as a diversion from the Judge Dominic Lynch delisting debacle, which severely threatened her position. The new Director of Prisons is the career civil servant who would almost certainly have succeeded to the post if it had remained within the department. Informed critics of the system and representatives of the rehabilitative professions are conspicuously absent from the interim board, but vested interests, most especially the POA, are well ensconced.

The huge expansion of prison places is the result not of a carefully conceived development plan aimed at improving the system, but of an unseemly Dutch auction by the political parties at the last general election. Political parties vied with each other over who would build more prison places in a campaign driven by Minister John O'Donoghue's vote-catching, strident 'law and order' and 'zero tolerance' rhetoric. It is clear that the expansion of prison places is primarily about making Ireland a more punitive and repressive society and decidedly not about improving prison conditions and bringing order and rationality to the penal system.

An irrefutable proof that the era of political neglect and indifference to the real problems of the penal system is not past are the atrociously low standards to which the new remand prison at Clover Hill has been built. This prison, which is for unconvicted, that is legally innocent, people, should set the 'gold standard' for conditions. This prison is also supposed to facilitate the general raising of standards throughout the system.

However, Clover Hill is itself designed to standards that are in significant respects well below those that pertained in the original Victorian prisons. The prison designed to solve the overcrowding problem has severe overcrowding deliberately built into its own design.

Cells in the Victorian Mountjoy Prison, designed for one person, were over 8 square metres in area. In the new human warehouse at Clover Hill, cells are about 11 square metres, less than 50 per cent larger, but are designed to be occupied by three people. Three hundred and sixty prisoners are to be housed in these triple cells. There are only twenty single cells and a small number of double cells (the attached Assessment Centre has forty single cells). There will be sanitation integral to the cells, but this means that legally innocent people will be forced to share an extremely confined space not just with two other people but with a toilet in the corner that is in fairly constant use. Beds are shorter than normal to fit the confined space and prisoners will eat from a table squeezed under the raised, third bunk bed. These formally innocent prisoners will spend at least sixteen hours a day locked up in their cells. Facilities for occupation for the extremely short out-of-cell period are poor, stretching to TV rooms, a weight-training gym, a small library, three domestic-science classrooms and a computer room for over 400 men. Remand prisoners, as officially innocent people, are allowed daily visits, if only for fifteen minutes. In Clover Hill visiting facilities make a presumption of guilt, since they separate visitors and prisoners by a total screen, thus precluding touching and any sense of personal contact or privacy. To further underline the diminished, isolated status of the remand prisoner, a court has been built adjacent to the prison. The court, which stands just outside the prison walls, is accessed by prisoners through an underground tunnel. The court is technically in the public domain, but from the prisoners' perspective it is now part of the prison. This new arrangement could, arguably, be said to breach the prisoners constitutional rights to have all aspects of procedure against them heard in public.

Studies have shown that remand prisoners are especially vulnerable to suicide[76]. Studies have also shown that a degree of privacy and a sense of personal security are two of the most important aspects of the prison climate for prisoners, essential to their mental and emotional well-being.[77] In this context, Clover Hill would appear to be a recipe for disaster that clearly sets an appallingly low standard for the design of prisons for well into the next century.

What matters most from the points of view of the prisoner and of the ordinary citizen, who cares about how the state treats its prisoners, are the prevailing conditions and the quality of regimes in the prisons. People who wish to see decent conditions for all prisoners can take little comfort from a development such as Clover Hill Prison. In the past, expansion of prison places has merely led to the expansion of the numbers held without any notable impact on prevailing conditions and regimes. Indeed, as the size of the prison population has increased, conditions and services have manifestly deteriorated in many areas. In the absence of the kind of radical rethinking of the whole penal process, for which I have argued, it is unreasonable to expect the present expansion to 4,000 places to be any different.

If past experience is anything to go by, and it is usually the best predictor of the future, expansion will not eradicate poor conditions, but will continue to coexist with unacceptable conditions and a very poor level of services and, no doubt, with extraordinary overtime budgets for prison officers. A prison population of 4,000 will more truly reflect the punitive overuse of imprisonment by the Irish courts, but, ironically, the system may still be overcrowded, because the courts have responded to the political demand for greater repression of visible crime, even at a time when recorded crime rates are notably declining. In the meantime, yet another symptom of persistent neglect, the totally obsolete 1947 Prison Rules[78] remain unrevised and continue to define and regulate prison regimes, insofar as that is any longer a practical possibility.

Enlightened managerialism is a failed entity in the penal system. It has recently grown in sophistication and subtlety, learning the benefits of public expression of a commitment to proper conditions and services. But it has always lacked the determination and vision – the sense of principled, informed moral commitment – to introduce obviously necessary reforms and services at anything but a token level, most useful for cosmetic, public-relations purposes.

The recent useful, but often superficial, reforms do not penetrate to the roots of the problem. Nor do they provide convincing evidence that the system is making a real effort to disperse the clouds of ignorance and secrecy that have obscured its activities in the past. Most importantly, there is little evidence of any new urgency to understand, analyse, and report on its own operations with the kind of clarity, precision and honesty that is required for effective forward-planning and genuine democratic accountability. The requirement to produce an annual report seems to have been conveniently forgotten.

The core problem of the overuse and misuse of imprisonment, that is the disproportion in Irish society's scale of punishment, remains unaddressed. In 1985, when the Whitaker Committee made its impassioned and timely plea for extending and strengthening non-custodial sanctions, there were 169 probation and welfare officers and 1,561 prison officers. Astoundingly, today, there are still only around 200 Probation and Welfare Officers, but 2,700 Prison Officers. The sincerity of the system's attempts to expand non-custodial options, both in the intervening years and at present, and its mindless attachment to incarceration as the main solution to crime are clearly illustrated by the fact that 400 new prison officers are currently to be recruited, while the Probation and Welfare Service has had to take industrial action to force the appointment of a miserly 39 new officers. Our political masters are still clearly failing to seriously address and prioritise the manifold problems of the penal system.

6. Social justice and the penal system

I have concentrated so far on an orthodox analysis of the problems of the Irish prison system, conceived in common-sense terms as a system for the reduction of crime and the protection of society. I have also focused on conditions in prison because, by its own account and, supposedly, by general agreement, the system has a paramount duty to realise its crime-reductive goals in a manner that respects fundamental human rights and the dignity of the individual offender.

I have argued that the system manifestly fails to inflict punishment that is restricted solely to the loss of liberty, but instead heaps a multitude of deprivations, dangers and degradations on the heads of prisoners and, in many cases, their families. Not for all, but for many Irish prisoners, prison life is a travesty of its own basic goal of a secure, caring environment, operating under and within the law. For many prisoners, the reality of life in the custody of the state is in crucial ways: not safe; not caring; not ordered; not law-abiding; and not rehabilitative. As a core social system dedicated to the pursuit of justice and the elimination of crime, prison is also an abject failure – largely ineffectual at the reduction of crime and riddled with incoherence and unfairness. As an expensive social project funded by the taxpayer, seemingly for the public good, it is disastrously mismanaged, inefficient, and unaccountable. The divergence between the expected effects and the actual effects of the prison system – the immense disparity between how things could be and should be and how they are – is plain for everyone to see.

But beyond these very grave concerns and the obvious agenda for immediate, practical reform arising from them, there are other problems that go to the heart of the question about the moral standing and legitimacy of the Irish penal system. The most relevant evidence on these problems concerns, on the one hand, the type of people Irish society chooses to process through the prison system and, on the other, what the system achieves with them in respect of their disposition to offend.

The question of the legitimacy of state punishment is customarily posed as the search for justification for the deliberate infliction of harm by an all-powerful state on relatively powerless individuals. If this harm was not officially labelled as punishment and did not claim useful and justifiable purposes, it would, clearly, be cruel, arbitrary and morally repugnant. As Macauley[79] said: 'The suffering caused by punishment is, considered by itself, an evil, and ought to be inflicted only for the sake of some prepondering good.' Justification at this level is invariably couched in terms of the instrumental purposes behind single instances of state punishment. These purposes will be examined in a later section but they can be conveniently summarised in terms of two broad themes – social defence against deviant individuals, who break society's rules, and gaining justice for the victims of crime. In other words, punishment is considered necessary for the prospective purpose of reducing the incidence of future crime and the retrospective purpose of rebalancing social relationships disturbed by crime (righting past wrongs).

But it can be argued that the prison system requires to be justified not alone in respect of its specific acts of punishment, but also in respect of its more general social effects, especially its role in maintaining the *status quo* within society. Taking the lead from the kind of criticism of prisons expressed by Durkheim and Foucault, the possibility must be addressed that the system deserves to be condemned because it covertly operates as a mechanism for the suppression of the angry, resisting dispossessed of society on behalf of the middle and upper classes, who are in firm possession of society's benefits and advantages. Arguably, those who control and benefit from the *status quo* are committed to using the apparatus of state punishment in order to remain in control. A judge of the High Court, Mr Justice Robert Barr, speaking at a conference in April 1999,[80] explained the kernel of the problem very succinctly. With surprising directness and candour – for a senior member of the Irish judiciary – he stated that the greatest injustice in contemporary Irish life is our failure as a caring society to take sufficient steps to rescue from crime those who are born to it and have the misfortune of existence without reasonable support in the marginalised, economically and socially deprived fringes of our society.

The most important evidence on this issue, then, concerns who is punished by imprisonment in Irish society and, as a corollary, who is not so punished despite their crimes. It is beyond dispute that a hugely disproportionate number of inmates of Irish prisons are born into the bleak, working-class and underclass, urban estates, which are characterised by poverty, chronic unemployment, substance-abuse problems, family disruption, poor and overcrowded housing, and severely curtailed opportunities for social and economic advancement.

Poverty, adverse social conditions and a pervasive sense of hopelessness and helplessness undermine the capacity of parents to raise their children to be well-adjusted, law-abiding, successful participants in society. Furthermore, the harsh psychological experience of being born into a stigmatised, socially inferior role and excluded from many of society's benefits – which the children of the middle-class receive as a birthright – leads to an adversarial mentality that is rejecting of the dominant middle-class moral order and often tolerant of dishonest means for acquiring otherwise unattainable material goods.

Many people rise above the severe disadvantages of poverty, perhaps earning a less meagre stake in society for themselves, but, regardless of their financial success or failure, maintaining a respectable, law-abiding lifestyle. But many from a stigmatised, deprived background gravitate towards crime as a means of survival in a highly competitive, acquisitive and materialistic society. They turn to crime as an escape from the boredom and oppression of their allotted social position. They turn to crime as a means to establish, however perversely, a sense of personal power and worth in a social context that tells them they are powerless and worthless.

It comes as no surprise that very many offenders and especially prisoners have failed drastically in the educational system. Most have failed to establish themselves in rewarding employment and have turned to alcohol and drugs to soothe their feelings of insecurity, inferiority and meaninglessness. In addition, many of them, having suffered a materially and emotionally deprived, often tragic and abusive, childhood, have severe difficulties in their adult personal relationships, lead chaotic lives, and experience profound mental and emotional problems. The deprived background and personal history of adversity and maladjustment that characterise the majority of Irish prisoners are not coincidental facts but strong indicators of the important causal contribution of the social environment to their criminality.

With few exceptions, such as cases of sex offending and murder, in which perpetrators tend to come from all classes, almost the full weight of Ireland's highly punitive penal system is directed at the repression of people from disadvantaged backgrounds and negligent, dysfunctional families – people who have failed in many areas of life, but most especially in the educational system that is now the chief key to success. Offenders often lack the special talents and personal attributes that would enable them to readily overcome the handicaps of their background and succeed in legitimate ways, but they always have some talents and positive attributes that have been cruelly inhibited by lack of opportunity and denied essential nurturance by an indifferent educational and social system.

Criminal behaviour is learned behaviour, and while the influence of social deprivation on crime is indirect and is mediated by powerful individual, family and situational factors, at the aggregate level of analysis, it is clear that, under present conditions, the prevalence of *visible* crime in Irish society is ultimately determined by the social environment and the lessons it teaches. People rarely begin by choosing crime, as it were as the best option for expressing their inner self, but rather drift into crime or graduate to it, step by step, because more positive ways to engage their energies and fulfil their desires and ambitions are unavailable to them.

Prison is clearly an hopelessly inadequate response to Judge Barr's call to rescue from crime those people born to it. Indeed, to the contrary, the evidence suggests that prison has become an important element in the social environment that fosters and perpetuates crime. In Ireland, prison rarely succeeds at reforming criminals or deterring them from crime, but more frequently confirms them in their criminal attitudes, aggravates their personal problems and escalates their criminal lifestyles. We have seen that prison is brought to bear largely on this most underprivileged sector of society mainly for relatively trivial, non-violent property offences. A large number of young people from the underclass are even sent to prison on their very first conviction for a petty offence.[81]

In Ireland, the extent of the overuse of imprisonment against minor offences is extraordinary, but the concentration of the disadvantaged amongst prisoners is also far greater than in other countries.[82] Not surprisingly, the evidence that the disproportionate and disorganised use of imprisonment against these people does not work, but is, on the contrary, counterproductive, is overwhelming. Ireland has one of the highest recidivism rates in the developed world. A recent study[83] indicated that the average Mountjoy prisoner had been in prison under conviction on nine different occasions. The record of the industrial schools, reformatories and detention centres, such as St Patrick's, is particularly appalling in this regard, indicating that they tend to operate as preparatory schools for serious criminals.

It is difficult to overstate the criminogenic effects of these juvenile institutions and of prisons in general. They tend to bond offenders together in an alliance that is aimed at rejecting their rejecters – in the person of prison staff, the police and the public at large. Prisoners build a counterculture that rationalises and glamorises crime and that values individual toughness and resistance above all else. The severe social stigma attached to being an ex-offender and the failure of the system to impact in positive ways on the personal development of offenders, through training, occupation, therapy and education, leave the prisoner in an even worse situation on release. If the services in prison are poor, the provision of post-release support is almost non-existent. The penal process is akin to mapping out a progressive career path for the criminal, by closing off legitimate opportunities and pushing him towards ever more serious criminal involvement.

The harsh physical and psychological conditions within prison and the prevalent negative public attitudes to offenders combine to send to prisoners a clear message of profound rejection and devaluation. From the prisoner's point of view this message is unjust and incomprehensible and must be denied.

We have lived through an era of revisionism that has witnessed the emergence of new, more sensitive attitudes in many areas, typified by the way that a whole vocabulary of exclusion and condemnation has become unacceptable. The withering of the use of terms like 'whore', 'bastard', 'lunatic', 'cretin', 'tinker', and 'queer' signals a significant evolution of public attitudes to a whole series of formerly despised and feared groups. Only the term 'criminal' remains absolutely respectable and retains its power to definitively stigmatise and exclude.

Of course, offenders are a real source of danger and fear and are perceived as deserving of blame because they have made criminal choices. But the main point I am making is that 'criminal' and 'prisoner' are what the sociologists call master roles; once ascribed, such roles are exceedingly difficult to shake off. The master role of 'criminal' tends to dictate societal reaction and to exercise a powerful and inescapable influence on an individual's psychology and life course. A penal system that imposes the status of 'prisoner' on minor offenders, who have often begun offending because society has failed to address their most basic needs, is indiscriminate, unnecessarily harsh, inevitably ineffective and morally questionable.

The credibility and force of this argument are greatly strengthened by one more, crucial fact about the Irish criminal justice system. This is that the system is almost exclusively focused on what I have called *visible* crime, crimes against the person and against property, such as larceny and robbery. These are the crimes of the typically deprived and disadvantaged 'criminal classes'. Very decidedly, the criminal justice and prison systems are not seriously deployed against the crimes of other sectors of Irish society.

Yet crime is by no means a monopoly of the 'criminal classes'. The Beef Tribunal[84] and the current Moriarty and Flood Tribunals have produced a wealth of evidence about the dishonesty and depredations of powerful and privileged individuals and corporations in Irish society. As Ciaran McCullagh[85] argues, society trivialises this kind of crime by means of weak legislation, inadequate mobilisation of law enforcement and inappropriately lenient sanctions.

There can be little doubt that so-called 'white-collar' crime is very widespread in Ireland and involves the dishonest appropriation of amounts of money and property that put the ill-gotten gains of *visible* crime into the half-penny place. The forms of this usually well-hidden criminality range widely across, for example, fraud, embezzlement, financial scams, insider trading, tax evasion, bribery and the corrupt use of political power. The most serious cases involve those in significant positions of power and trust and those with access to large amounts of money, but the incidence of 'white-collar' offences is widespread and includes numerous petty offences, such as expense-fiddling. Much of this crime remains hidden because it is successful; but research[86] shows that the majority of the crime that is detected is dealt with outside the criminal justice system by institutions wary of bad publicity that might undermine public trust in them. It is a bitter irony that the vast majority of the few thousand 'white-collar' type crimes, that are processed annually, are the minor misdemeanours of the 'criminal classes'. These are small-scale cases of prescription forgery, cheque-passing, social welfare fraud and the like. As Swift[87] wrote: 'Laws are like cobwebs, which may catch small flies, but let wasps and hornets break through'.

However, the phenomenon of ignored and 'invisible' crime is not confined to crimes of financial dishonesty but covers conduct such as drunk driving, domestic violence and corporate abuse of the environment and flouting of health and safety regulations. A case can be made that these crimes add immeasurably more to the sum of human unhappiness than the *visible* crimes that are targeted by the system[88]. The example of sex abuse of children and women is especially pertinent. In recent years this type of crime, which takes a terrible toll on victims, has at last been exposed and the full power of the criminal justice system has been mobilised against it. Now almost one in eight of Irish prisoners are sex offenders. This category includes people from all classes and walks of life. Yet only a small proportion of sex offenders are actually prosecuted and punished by the criminal justice system. This is the case mainly because only a minority of sex offences are reported to the police[89]. It is clear that, if all those people committing sex offences and the various other types of *invisible* crime, such as fraud, occupational crime and domestic violence, were properly punished, the composition of the prison population would be transformed beyond all recognition. There is little doubt that, in such a situation, the complacency and ambivalence about prison conditions and about the use of prison that currently permeate public attitudes would be substantially diminished.

At present, the prison system operates to reinforce feelings of social distance from those who are already held at a remote social distance – in the words of Nils Christie[90] 'making it easier not to feel scruples about inflicting punishment.' A prison population that reflected the whole spectrum of the Irish population, that included the fathers, sons and brothers of the middle-classes, would, I suggest, be treated in a much more humane and constructive manner.

While these facts cast doubts over the wider legitimacy of the penal system, they do not imply that we must excuse criminal behaviour on the basis of a background of severe socio-economic disadvantage but rather that we must cease excusing criminal behaviour linked to power and relative privilege. Claudius in Shakespeare's *Hamlet* shows himself to be astutely aware of how the power which was the fruit of his regicide enabled him to evade justice: 'In the corrupted currents of this world, offence's gilded hand may shove by justice; and oft tis seen the wicked prize itself buys out the law'. It is clearly often the case in Ireland that the power of money and status provide an opaque screen both for crime and the evasion of punishment.

The criminal justice system must hold all individuals responsible for their criminal conduct, for the most part, regardless of their personal background and of the causes of that conduct. As Philip Bean[91] states: 'the law is an institution designed to give people artificial motives for respecting the interests of others'. This means that the law is the ultimate instrument for defining and sanctioning unacceptable behaviours, an instrument which must come into play when subjective controls, such as conscience, ingrained inhibitions and empathy, and normal social constraints fail. However, blaming and punishing individual criminals cannot succeed or be fully justified, if it is done selectively with respect to both offences and types of offender. Moreover, blaming and punishing individuals is at best a partial solution, which will fail, if broader society does not simultaneously confront the disequilibrium in its own structure that helps mould the *visible* criminal and his behaviour.

We must acknowledge and act on the fact that the lack of effective distributive justice in society and continuing gross, social inequalities play a significant role in the genesis of *visible* crime. As Barbara Hudson[92] explains:

> If it remains confined within its present parameters, penal discourse offers little hope of altering the differential impact of penal policy on rich and poor, black and white, conventional and unconventional. Just as penal policy can only have a minimal impact on crime without broader social strategies of crime prevention, so it can have little impact on justice without broader policies to reduce inequalities and social divisions, and to increase social provision.

Indeed, it can be argued, along with Judge Barr, that a penal system, which selectively enforces laws in society and does not genuinely struggle to correct its own structural inequalities, is not merely illegitimate but is itself a major source of social injustice.

I have argued, then, that the legitimacy of the Irish penal system is undermined by 1) unjustly harsh prison conditions and inadequate or totally absent services, which together further disadvantage and devalue socially excluded prisoners and, occasionally, seriously contravene their basic human rights; 2) rejecting public attitudes that further alienate and marginalise prisoners, who have from birth been denied a fair stake in society; 3) inappropriate use of imprisonment that widens the net to unnecessarily expose minor and young offenders to the criminal counterculture and the other pernicious effects of prison; 4) unfair use of imprisonment, such as arbitrary or politically motivated early release of selected prisoners, that introduces an element of serious injustice into the system and so destroys any possibility that the prisoner might recognise the justice of his own punishment; and 5) the failure of the criminal justice system to seriously confront whole areas of *invisible* crime that are attributable to all social classes or, in the case of lucrative 'white-collar' crime, especially to the more powerful and privileged.

These five sources of injustice are, of course, intimately related to the underlying problem of social injustice. Irish society maintains the kind of penal system it has, precisely because it is a deeply divided and unequal society. Ambivalent attitudes to 'white-collar' crime and the failure to root out corruption, major financial dishonesty and other very harmful types of *invisible* crime coexist with repressive 'law and order' rhetoric and vigorous, enthusiastic action against *visible* crime. These conflicting approaches are intrinsic to a system that privileges and, in a sense, has been designed to privilege the 'haves' over the 'have-nots'. As Mathiesen[93] argues, 'the heavy-handed use of prison against traditional criminals from the lower working class diverts our attention from the dangers flowing from those in power.' The acts and omissions of the criminal justice and penal system are inextricably linked to the realities of social division, first, because they are conditioned by these realities and, second, because they help perpetuate them. On this interpretation, the penal system must be considered one of the most flagrant and outrageous symptoms of the deep-rooted hypocrisy of Irish society.

The most important conclusion from this analysis is that the pursuit of a just society in the sense of a society free of crime is indivisible from the pursuit of a just society in the sense of a society that is fair and equitable in its distribution of opportunities and constraints, benefits and burdens. It is not mere idealism, but a moral and pragmatic necessity that we begin to construct a criminal justice and penal system on the foundations of a genuinely more egalitarian, political vision for society.

The roots and basis of state punishment

Having made this key point about the centrality of social justice to the legitimacy of criminal justice, it will be useful to take, briefly, a more philosophical and historically aware point of view that permits acknowledgement of both the underlying necessity for prison and the strengths of the present penal system, most particularly the checks and balances on the powers of the system which have evolved over recent centuries. This will be useful because it is essential to recognise that an attack on our penal system, based on its inherent lack of social justice, does not imply that society can or should survive without prisons. It will also be useful because it is equally essential to recognise and appreciate the extent to which the Irish criminal justice and penal system already strives for and in part attains legitimacy.

There are four major issues here: 1) the reality and the basis of the state's intrinsic power and right to punish; 2) the methodology for justifying punishing a specific individual; 3) the methodology for justifying punishing to a given degree; and 4) the control of the actuality of punishment, involving a limited degree of protection for the punished by means of a legally enforceable human rights machinery. In order to elucidate these

issues, especially in relation to current popular and political attitudes, which act as a barrier to the kind of progress I am
advocating, I will briefly examine the remote historical roots of
our current criminal and penal system in this section and issues
2 to 4 in the following section.

Our current criminal justice and penal system can be seen, as
I have argued, as an imperfect system with very serious flaws.
But, from an historical perspective, the system can be correctly
regarded as a transitional work-in-progress, which represents, in
many respects, a remarkable advance on previous methods for
maintaining social order. Our present system embodies many
effective mechanisms that are primarily designed to assure its
own legitimacy. It is important to remember that without these
mechanisms and the genuine if qualified legitimacy they confer,
without this history of progress, it would not be possible to even
frame the broader question of the legitimacy of the criminal
justice and penal system in relation to social justice.

Penal activity, that is some type of formal punishment by
recognised authorities within a society, is a universal feature of
all human societies, including relatively primitive groups.
Socially organised and ordained punishment initially replaced
private revenge-taking by victims or their kinsmen and was an
essential step in the direction of a more cohesive, structured and
developed society. For example, the anthropologists, Freeman
and Winch,[94] studied forty-eight human groups and societies at
different stages of development, from isolated stone-age, hunter-
gatherer type groups through early settled agricultural groups
and onwards. They found that the invention of a formal system
for resolving disputes, recognising harm done to undeserving
victims and inflicting punishment on perpetrators, was one of
the earliest and most crucial steps in the development of society.
Groups and communities that did not have a system of organised
punishment rarely had full-time priests and groups that had no
full-time priests tended not to progress to the point of having
dedicated educators. In short, some kind of organised social
regulation, some agreed or at least acquiesced-in system of

judicial and penal authority is a necessary precondition for the emergence of a stable social group.

There is a volatile potential for anarchy, disruption and disintegration endemic in the human endeavour to live co-operatively. Man is obviously a social animal and early tribal societies, which evolved for the mutual benefit of members, were undoubtedly extensions of the naturally cohesive family system. However, there is considerable controversy in philosophy and political theory about the genesis of the state and about the relationship between the individual and the state.[95] Arguments centre on issues such as whether the state should be regarded as an organism superior to the individual or as a mechanical device, designed to serve individuals, or whether the relationship between individual and state is underpinned by consent or by force. Whatever one's position on these issues, it is inconceivable that primitive, stable communities of the type that have given rise to modern states could have emerged without first and foremost finding organisational solutions to the problems posed by wrong-doing and violent disputes. While the benefits of co-operative living in terms of sociability, survival and security may have been the motivational wellsprings for the creation of early tribal societies, the first task must have been to cement people together by finding ways to defuse disputes, which had the potential to split loyalties and fragment the incipient community.

Punishment by the social group, then, is ultimately justified by two core purposes. The grounding purpose is for the collective in the person of its designated representatives – in primitive societies usually patriarchal tribal leaders and elders – to act as the avenging agent for wronged individuals. As Swinburne[96] argues 'the primary justification of punishment is as a substitute for revenge in circumstances where it is better that some authority act as the agent of the victim in exacting his revenge'.

However, immediately the collective embarks on this process there is an inescapable need to ensure that the new penal process is undertaken in a way that creates and maintains consistent, predictable and orderly social authority. As Cicero[97] states: 'laws were invented for the safety of citizens and for the preservation of states'. Systems of punishment are rooted in the need to develop and enforce a set of rules governing how humans live together, but once a regulatory system is in place, the system of collective punishment itself becomes one of the principal sites of social authority and a chief means by which a society asserts and assures its own cohesion and continuity. The system of collective punishment is simultaneously a practical solution to the social disruptiveness of wrong-doing, a symbol of the cohesion of a society and the chief means by which that society exercises collective power. The second core purpose underpinning punishment by the social group, therefore, is the need to protect the authority to punish, once it has been granted. This purpose, essentially identifiable with the preservation of the state – that is the new order of values and the organisational structures for the exercise of power – is constructed on but quickly takes precedence over the ontologically prior purpose of acting as the avenging agent for wronged individuals.

It is necessary for the social collective to exact revenge precisely because only in this way can the continuity and solidarity of the group be maintained and strengthened, rather than jeopardised and disrupted. The transition to collective punitive action is motivated by the grounding purpose of replacing the cycle of vindictive blood-letting, which will fragment a community, with an orderly system of measured revenge-taking, which will hold it together. However, this grounding purpose is in the process of its own implementation quickly subordinated to the wider purpose of creating, representing and maintaining the new system of social order generally. The system of judicial and penal authority is required to maintain solidarity, but it must inevitably face and meet all challenges to its own authority and, of course, it has been granted the power to do so.

A pragmatic necessity to punish wrong-doing and substitute social regulation for the potentially ruinous disruption of personal revenge-taking undergirds the state's right and power to punish. In a sense, the birth of the state can be identified with the moment of successful transition from a disorganised system of personal vengeance to one of orderly punishment by the collective (with the consent or at least acquiescence of both victim and perpetrator). The state's very existence is predicated upon its assumption of the authority to maintain order and continuity through rule-setting and the punishment of rule-breaking. Conversely, the right and power of the state to punish flows ineluctably from the existence of the state. Although specific instances of state punishment can be challenged in many ways from a moral standpoint, it would be ludicrous to challenge the general right of the state to regulate and to punish violations of its regulations.

Penal authority, therefore, is at the very centre of social life. It is not a newly forged product of democracy or of sophisticated modern social and political arrangements, rather it is a precondition for all social and political development. It is not, as often appears to be the case today, a minor, disregarded function of the state, an irritating diversion from the real business of society that would be dispensable but for a troublesome minority of intransigent offenders. When judicial and penal authority and the rule of law break down, as we have seen in states like the former Yugoslavia, anarchy reigns and the very identity and survival of the state is threatened or destroyed. Since an inability or unwillingness to enforce the regulations that govern key aspects of interpersonal behaviour and to exercise the right to punish threatens the existence of the state, one might even argue that the state is obliged to seek out and punish violations of its regulations.

Of course, as societies developed and became more complex, the connections between social authority, social regulation, force and the core activities of exacting a measured revenge in a benevolent, restorative manner and maintaining the organisational power structure of the state, became very complex. In developed social systems the basis of actual punishment in the grounding purpose of substituting for revenge often became extremely tenuous or totally obscured. In particular, as societies developed and social roles and divisions multiplied, the ability to define wrong-doing and inflict punishment rapidly became the sole prerogative of the powerful and so came to be regularly exploited and abused. Historically, state systems of punishment have more often than not upheld a blatantly unjust, oppressive social order and, from the ordinary citizen's point of view, were obviously more often an imposition by *force majeure* than a benign product of some, theoretically voluntary, social contract between individual and state. Even today, although democracy has effectively reshaped the criminal justice system so that it does offer some real protection to the individual against the awesome powers of the state, it is uncertain whether the ordinary citizen believes he or she has willingly entered a contract with the state or he or she feels totally powerless and coerced by their involuntary membership in society.

The evolution of 'due process', proportionality and human rights

No doubt, intuitive notions of justice and fair play have from the very beginning of organised social life been an important consideration in the penal process, but it is important to recognise that a legal framework, consciously designed to implement justice for all parties to the process, is a relatively recent innovation. Our present system of criminal law has evolved over many centuries and has been shaped as much by the struggle to control the exercise of power in society as by the search for the ideal of justice between all people. It is arguable that, historically, the present legal concept of justice evolved mainly out of the attempt to manage power struggles between different individuals and between individuals and the collective and to regain citizens' consent to punishment imposed by social authorities.

We are now very familiar with systems of social and political authority which incorporate self-imposed limits and which confer specific rights on the individual. However, these are recent developments which have been hard won and have superseded systems in which the authorities exercised absolute, untrammeled power over the individual. As little as a few hundred years ago, authorities everywhere, were able to inflict punishments of the most torturous, cruel and disproportionate nature without let or hindrance. One does not have to go very far back in history to find a time when a sovereign, chieftain or member of a ruling elite, secular or religious, was empowered to punish subject members of society without any valid proof of wrong-doing or indeed, sometimes, without any reference to guilt. These conditions still prevail in certain societies today and some societies, which we consider as among the most advanced, such as Germany, have suffered recent periods of reversion to barbaric standards of law with appalling consequences that equal or exceed the worst atrocities of, for example, the feudal or inquisition eras.

Concepts, such as the rule of law, equality before the law, judicial independence and human rights, inspired the rise of democracy. But their realisation in our present legal structures derived from and depended on the success of the struggle for democracy. There have been many important landmarks on the road to our present relatively positive situation, such as the Magna Carta, the American Declaration of Independence, the French Revolution and the eventual emergence of parliamentary representative power.

With respect to punishment, the two most important products of the gradual, progressive evolution of law are 'due process' and the principle of proportionality, which both place limits on society's power to punish. 'Due process' addresses the justification for punishing a specific individual and the principle of proportionality addresses the justification for punishing to a given degree. Both are methods for redressing the immense imbalance of power between individuals and the social authorities, which exercise the power to punish. 'Due process' and proportionality of punishment have been embodied in the law to protect the individual, because it has come to be recognised that it is wrong to knowingly punish the innocent or crush the minor offender with extreme and harsh measures, even if such punishments can be justified as in the best interests of society or its more powerful members.

'Due process', including the explicit definition of criminal conduct, the presumption of innocence and the adoption of fair procedures to govern trials, evidence-giving and interrogation, is a relatively straightforward matter of arranging that any specific judgment of guilt and culpability shall be made only after certain steps have been taken to maximise the likelihood that the judgement will be a correct and fair one. 'Due process' is clearly not tied to always being right in the making of judgments of guilt, but rather to always taking a defined degree of care in the making of such judgments. Errors can be expected in the application of 'due process' but they do not of themselves invalidate the procedure, which remains one of the most precious features of our civilisation.[98]

Proportionality in sentencing is a somewhat vaguer and more vexed matter, but it is essentially concerned with restricting punishment to the degree appropriate to the seriousness of the offence and the culpability of the offender. It is also necessarily concerned with maintaining relativities between punishments handed down for similar offences or for similarly culpable offenders. The utilitarian principle of parsimony,[99] which states that punishment should be the minimum consistent with the crime-reductive goals of punishment, is a related principle that is also influential in sentencing practice. Both principles can be seen as vital contributions to the law, which enable the system to part justify its own punitive powers by placing limits on them.

Although 'due process' and proportionality represent crucially important advances for our civilisation, their influence is confined largely to the abstract calculation of just deserts and they do not impact significantly on the practical means by which punishment is implemented, such as the conditions of imprisonment. In this century, a separate, powerful tool has been developed to help ensure the appropriateness of punishment as it actually bears on the prisoner. This is the legally enforceable machinery of human rights. Human rights, such as the right to life or the right to privacy, are derived from a principled commitment to treat human life and the dignity of the individual human being with genuine respect. Human rights, as enshrined in international conventions and national constitutions, have a universal application, transcending the interests of powerful political and social institutions and vested groups.

With respect to prisoners, progress in this area translates into a recognition that the imprisoned retain all human rights not automatically circumscribed by the loss of liberty.[100] Legal measures for the vindication of human rights now provide an effective means of protection against the more extreme forms of maltreatment, such as torture, starvation, and cruel and unusual punishment or treatment. However, unfortunately, the focus of the human rights machinery is firmly on preventing and remedying excessively brutal treatment and its capacity to effect positive change in and guarantee the humanity of prison regimes is weak and, as yet, little more than aspirational.

The instrumental purposes of punishment and the necessity for prison

Over recent centuries, a philosophical and jurisprudential discourse about the instrumental purposes of state punishment has developed in parallel with the evolution of mechanisms for the protection of the individual against the overweening powers of the state, which I have just described. In essence, the discourse on purposes is an ideological search for justification of acts of state punishment and an implicit recognition of the moral nature of such acts. While the mechanisms for the protection of individual rights, like 'due process', address certain aspects of the *how* of punishment, this discourse on the purposes of punishment addresses the *why*. But in the final analysis, the *how* and *why* questions cannot be kept separate, because ideologies about the purpose of punishment exert an enormous influence over the concrete organisation and application of punishment. Views on why we punish inevitably influence the everyday reality of imprisonment which, I have argued, goes largely untouched by 'due process', proportionality and the human rights machinery.

The common understanding of why the state punishes (and the purposes behind judicial sentencing) is well expressed in the report of the National Crime Forum.[101] The report describes the purposes of prison as 'to protect society by keeping dangerous criminals out of circulation; to indicate society's abhorrence of the crime; to deter criminal action; to punish such action when it has been committed; and to rehabilitate the criminal.' In the philosophical and jurisprudential literature on punishment[102] these instrumental purposes of punishment are conventionally termed, respectively, the incapacitative, the declaratory or expressive, the deterrent (working on both the individual offender and the general population), the retributive or punitive, and the reform or rehabilitative.

The discourse on purposes focuses on single acts of punishment for specific violations of the criminal law. It therefore presupposes a social consensus on the definition of wrongdoing. Because of this narrowed focus, there is no overt reference to the grounding purpose of state punishment, that is the substitution of orderly, measured revenge for victim revenge. But this underlying purpose has clearly been sublimated into the purpose of retribution, the view that a wrong must be punished – must be expiated by the wrong-doer – in order to rebalance the social relationships disturbed by crime.

Equally, reference to the overarching objective of ensuring the continuity of social authority and order and protecting the *status quo* is indirect. But this intrinsic property of state punishment is clearly implicit in all five instrumental purposes that constitute the discourse. The role of punishment in the maintenance of the *status quo* is most obvious in respect of the declaratory purpose, which can be understood as the use of the criminal justice and penal system for the expression and enforcement of the framework of values and rules, to which society wishes its members to conform. It is also implicit in the other purposes, for example, the goal of reform presupposes the code of socially ordained values and acceptable conduct, to which a reformed individual is expected to conform.

There is considerable theoretical controversy about the different instrumental purposes. In particular, the reform and retributive goals are often thought to be contradictory and mutually destructive. As G.B. Shaw[103] succinctly puts it 'to punish a man you must injure him, to reform a man you must improve him, and men are not improved by injuries'. The philosophical argument can be briefly summarised as a conflict between the utilitarian view that stresses the consequences of punishment and measures success in terms of the impact on the sum of human happiness and the Kantian view that stresses the autonomy and moral responsibility of the individual and asserts the moral imperative to punish a past wrong. The utilitarian perspective sees punishment as a means to the end of reducing crime, while the Kantian perspective sees punishment as an end in itself, unrelated to social objectives like the reduction of crime.

It is difficult to see how these conflicting positions can be reconciled, but influential modern thinkers, like David Garland,[104] argue that it is inappropriate to adhere to a single instrumental purpose for punishment. Punishment by the state, they believe, must rely simultaneously on all five justificatory purposes, notwithstanding the contradictions between those purposes. So, for example, punishment by imprisonment is normally motivated by a set of mixed purposes – the deterrence and, at least temporary, incapacitation of the offender himself, deterrence of others by the example of his punishment and by the associated expression of social disapproval, reform of the offender, and a degree of punitive retaliation against the offender consistent with the harm caused by him.

This kind of mixture of purposes is unavoidable and indeed useful because the interplay of purposes can curb the excesses that arise when a single purpose is favoured. For example, the deterrent purpose is forward-looking and concerned fundamentally with the reduction of future crime. Without the moderating influence of the retributive purpose, which looks backwards at the seriousness of the offence and emphasises the moral dimensions of just deserts and proportionality, a focus on deterrence could lead to a regime of ever harsher punishments.

The past history of imprisonment is replete with examples of the failure of and the damage caused by single-purpose ideological views of punishment. For example, the penitentiaries of the early nineteenth century were designed on a religiously inspired, reform model. As Ignatieff[105] puts it, 'salvation was not only God's work. It was the State's work too, and for the first time a technology of salvation existed for earthly use'. The austere conditions, the religious milieu of daily services and ubiquitous biblical tracts, and the 'separate and silent' solitary confinement system of the penitentiary were explicitly intended to engineer the conversion of the criminal to a state of religious grace. This ideology rapidly collapsed because it manifestly failed to achieve genuine conversions or to prevent recidivism and because solitary confinement soon tipped many vulnerable prisoners over the edge into madness.

However, it was replaced with an even more dangerous ideology focused exclusively on the single purpose of deterrence. In 1863, Lord Chief Justice Cockburn[106] famously stated that : 'The primary object of the treatment of prison is deterrence, through suffering, inflicted as a punishment for crime, and the fear of the repetition of it'. This approach provided a rationale for the imposition of cruel conditions, such as hard, non-productive labour on the treadmill. An ascendant deterrent model encouraged the deliberate increase of the misery of prison life. It later led, in the US, to the totally disproportionate and crushingly harsh system of indeterminate sentences (for example, five to forty years for a relatively minor crime), which deprived prisoners of hope for the future. The ideological influence of a one-dimensional deterrence theory can still be seen today in the presence of the objectionable 'three strikes and out' laws, recently introduced in many US states. These laws allow for life sentences for repeated petty crime, including in one outlandish instance a life sentence resulting from the theft of a pizza[107].

The modern view that punishment must strive to simultaneously satisfy multiple purposes also serves as a credible answer to the trenchant arguments of abolitionists, who believe that prison's negative impact on social justice and prison's history of failure to achieve its instrumental purposes inevitably imply that society would be better off without prisons. Mathiesen,[108] for example, believes that prison is a 'fiasco in terms of its own purposes' and that for the future we must envisage further contraction and eventual abolition of prison because 'anything else is tantamount to acceding to irrationality'.

A case can be made for the abolition of prison based solely on the impressive accumulation of evidence that the prison fails to achieve either the reform or deterrence of the offender. This evidence has led to the 'nothing works' debate of recent decades[109] and the associated loss of faith in the possibility of effective rehabilitation. While this negative view of the potential for rehabilitation has been tempered by a resurgence of confidence, in the 1990s, and recent empirical proof[110] that carefully tailored and properly resourced, rehabilitative programmes can work, research findings generally show that community-based rather than prison-based programmes are more effective. Moreover, the success of prison (and community-based sanctions) at reducing recidivism remains marginal and can hardly be said to outweigh the criminogenic effects of the prison and its continuing role in promoting social inequality.

Yet the arguments for the abolition of prison finally fail to convince because they do not address the complex, multiple purposes of punishment and prison. In the first place, the retributive purpose stresses the need for punishment for its own sake – as an end in itself without reference to the consequences of punishment. Underlying this is the continuing importance of exacting a measured revenge on behalf of victims. This might be an unspoken purpose of punishment, but it is essential. The horrifying example of forms of rough justice in Northern Ireland –

punishment beatings and assassinations of 'ordinary' criminals by paramilitaries – and the spectacle of vindictive, violent retaliation linked to feuds within the travelling community are powerful testimony to the importance of state control of retribution.

In recent years in Dublin, vigilante groups have emerged and become involved in illegal retaliation against and coercion of drug-dealers. This is evidence of the ever-present danger of regression to blood-letting and illegitimate revenge-taking, whenever the state fails to intervene and exercise its legitimate and, as I have argued, necessary coercive powers. Similarly, the abolitionist argument fails to address the success of prison as an instrument for denunciation and for the expression of societal values and its possibly effective role in deterring the general population.

Most obviously of all, the abolitionist argument fails to confront the evident success of the prison at incapacitating offenders, at least temporarily. At this most practical level, it is inconceivable, given the seriousness of some criminal behaviour, that we could manage without prisons. In complex, modern societies that value individual freedom and well-being, there is, inevitably, enormous scope for ruthless people to take unfair advantage of vulnerable others and to harm them greatly. Many offences involve a level of vicious and violent conduct that destroys lives and demands a strongly punitive response. Many intransigent offenders are set in their criminal ways and are immune to conventional social disapproval and moral pressure to behave decently towards others, in accordance with the law. In the absence of corporal and capital punishment, prison is the only means of physical restraint available to society.

It is self-evidently reasonable and just that society use the coercion of prison to incapacitate persistent, serious wrong-doers. It also appears reasonable and just that society deprive people of their liberty in order to mark the seriousness of particularly aggressive and harmful offences, such as murder or rape, and in order to exact revenge on behalf of offenders' victims, even when there is little likelihood that the offence will be repeated.

While it is obviously right to look to prison to reduce crime and to reform offenders, it is necessary to concede that for other, distinct reasons, such as retribution, general deterrence, denunciation and mere incapacitation, prison is a necessary and useful response to certain types of crime, whether or not it does any reductive or reformative good in the specific case. A nuanced, comprehensive view of the role of prison must acknowledge this fact and must accommodate the related fact that, in Garland's words,[111] 'punishment is fated never to "succeed" to any great degree because the conditions which do most to induce conformity – or to promote crime and deviance – lie outside the jurisdiction of penal institutions'.

Holding people criminally responsible

The philosophical dilemmas around punishment are not confined to the questions of legitimacy and purposes. Equally important to an understanding of this highly complex process is the issue of blame and responsibility, which hinges on the philosophical argument about determinism and free will. The crux of this issue is in the contradiction between the fact that, subjectively, most rational human beings experience a sense of personal agency and autonomy – a sense that they shape their own lives even if in circumstances finally beyond their control – and the fact that when human conduct is made the subject of normal scientific explanation it inevitably appears to be determined by causes outside the control of the individual. As Nagel[112] states: 'Ultimately, nothing or almost nothing about what a person does seems to be under his control'.

This is an extremely difficult topic, argued at length in a voluminous literature.[113] But in the present context, the main point is that the criminal justice system works on a presumption of free will. In the absence of recognised mitigating factors, such as mental illness or duress, which undermine an offender's capacity to understand his own actions or intend them, the courts work on a presumption that the offender exercised free will in making his criminal choices, that he could have acted otherwise. The courts rely on this presumption as a kind of guillotine to cut off a potentially interminable debate about the causes of crime. The life history or social setting that shaped and determined criminal acts, including the influence of social deprivation and a dysfunctional upbringing, are, therefore, ultimately irrelevant.

In the final analysis, the courts must and do respond to criminal behaviours as the presumed result of free rational choice. Therefore, they strictly ignore the remote and more immediate external conditions that led to the behaviour and helped form the criminal intent. Any other approach would open the way for explanations that tend to dissolve responsibility and exonerate the perpetrator, because they construe him as a victim of uncontrollable circumstances.

This is how things must be, because the courts are primarily a prescriptive system, which plays an active role in the socialisation of anti-social or ineffectively socialised individuals. As von Hayek[114] puts it: 'we assign responsibility to a man, not in order to say that, as he was, he might have acted differently, but in order to make him different.' The criminal courts act in order to influence behaviour, by declaring which behaviours are intolerable to society, and by deploying sanctions to change people's attitudes and conduct in regard to these behaviours.

This approach – intrinsic to criminal law – is also consistent with our own subjective experience of being autonomous, responsible agents and our tendency to conceive conduct in terms of a strictly limited set of internal causes situated within the psychology of the individual. For example, motives like greed, lust, selfishness, aggression and self-indulgence almost by definition play a central part in many crimes. The law and people in general rarely look beyond such motives for the causes of wrongful conduct. With circular logic, we tend to explain criminal conduct in terms of personal character, motivation and personality.

Factors in the social environment that may have shaped individual character are ruled out by the guillotine of free will. The criminal justice and penal system is, then, engaged in a process which blames people for what they are and attributes what people do to what they are, but carefully excludes consideration of what made people what they are. This straightjacketed thinking is essential to the law and profoundly influences popular and political attitudes, making it much easier for people to ignore the role of social disadvantage in the genesis of *visible* crime. However, in our endeavour to construct a better society, we cannot afford to take this narrowed perspective.

Public and political attitudes that are an obstacle to recognition of the role of social justice in criminal justice

These points about the complexity of holding people accountable for their actions, about the clear necessity and justifiable rationale for prison, about the elusive quality of justice and about the centrality of procedures designed to assure the legitimacy of state punishment are important because they help explain public and political attitudes to the penal system and because they clarify the limits on what the criminal justice and penal system can be expected to achieve by way of substantiation of social justice. The philosophical complexity of the punishment process helps explain the general attitudinal ambivalence about the prisons, the lack of public concern for the moral quality of state punishment, and, in some quarters, the excessively blaming and punitive attitudes towards prisoners, which all underlie the chaotic, counterproductive and in many ways inhumane penal system that we have.

For example, it is a paradox that the existence of a human rights machinery and of mechanisms, such as 'due process' and the principle of proportionality, which are all designed to achieve just punishment, tends to lull society into a sense of complacency about the practical operation of the penal system. The fact that some effective safeguards are in place to protect the accused (from miscarriages of justice) and the convicted prisoner (from extreme forms of maltreatment) encourages inattention to the more mundane inadequacy and inhumanity of the actual means used to punish. It is worth expanding on these points about public and political attitudes in order to articulate some of the causes for societal indifference to the failures of the prison system and for the lack of political will to tackle the criminal justice and penal system's detrimental role in social justice.

As we have seen in the previous sections, punishment by the state is a complex moral transaction, involving a set of concepts and precepts, which tend, among other things, to direct attention away from the role of the social environment in crime. Overlaying this tendency and reinforcing it, is the powerful logic of the argument that many criminal acts cannot be sensibly related to social injustice and that many people who have suffered social deprivation and personal adversity do not get involved in crime.

The following arguments convince many people that it is fallacious to attribute even *visible* crime to social disadvantage:

- The fact that crime is very low amongst some socially and economically disadvantaged groups. In particular, as recent studies have shown many of the most disadvantaged people live in rural areas[115] and have very low crime rates. This argument can be extended to cover the fact that women, who often bear the worst pains of deprivation, tend to be law-abiding, even in the most dreadful of material circumstances.
- The fact that people, such as brothers, brought up in very similar, deprived environments may differ totally with respect to crime, avoiding it or embracing it.
- The fact that a relatively small minority of the marginalised sector of society, a minority which is not representative of its class, accounts for a huge proportion of crime.
- The fact that there is an immense amount of 'white collar crime', especially crimes of dishonesty, at all levels of society. These crimes are most commonly acquisitive crimes against property like most of the *visible* crime processed by the

criminal justice system and generally go unnoticed and unpunished, but they are clearly not related to social deprivation.

These arguments strongly suggest that social deprivation is not a direct or sole cause of crime, but they do not controvert the compelling evidence, already reviewed in this pamphlet, that social deprivation, albeit mediated by other factors, plays a pivotal role in the genesis of *visible* crime. What Judge Barr calls the greatest injustice in contemporary Irish life remains largely unchallenged. Neither do these arguments address the implications for social justice of the criminal justice and penal system's failure to confront *invisible* forms of crime. Unfortunately, many people ignore these realities and prefer to rely on the above arguments to discount altogether the role of social deprivation in crime. These superficial arguments, which gloss over the logical subtleties, play a negative role in fostering public indifference to the social injustice of the criminal justice and penal system.

Many other factors reinforce negative public and political attitudes. Imprisonment is a banishment, which itself consolidates public indifference and complacency. Prisoners are consigned to a form of internal exile – out of sight and out of mind. Moreover, imprisonment is regarded as a deserved, legitimate form of social exclusion, brought down on prisoners' heads by their own misconduct. This view harmonises with the still prevalent notion of 'less eligibility' – the idea that the imprisoned are less deserving than the least deserving of a society's unconvicted, innocent citizens[116] and should, therefore, be provided with less. Shaw[117] summarised the logic of the Victorian version of 'less eligibility' as follows: 'If the prison does not underbid the slum in human misery, the slum will empty and the prison will fill.' In our present society, there are many pockets of grossly inadequate health care and some dreadful conditions in residential homes for aged, mentally ill and disabled citizens. This means, on the one hand, that many people see an undeniable logic in the notion of the 'less eligible' prisoner, and, on the other, that the standards set for prisons by the criterion of 'less eligibility' are disastrously poor.

Also, the fact that imprisonment is an effective form of social exclusion is convenient for the majority of people who do not wish to know those who offend. But it means that they are never likely to understand why these people do offend or to fully grasp the key role of social deprivation in the causation of crime.

Public attitudes to punishment are further confused by the otherwise very welcome new emphasis on the role of the victim in the criminal process. Innovations such as victim-impact statements have considerable value for the frequently neglected victim, but they often stir intense emotions and provoke highly punitive reactions. Media-driven moral panics also often cause emotive, irrational reactions to crime to spread to large sectors of the population with no direct experience as victims. This in turn puts irresistible pressure on politicians to pursue apparently repressive policies.

Even the increased competitiveness of modern life has a part to play in the intensification of public reaction to crime. The sense that each of us is under extreme demands to perform and conform engenders a feeling that we deserve whatever gains we might have achieved.[118] The corollary of this is that we are prone to think that others deserve their failures and miseries. If the people suffering miserably happen to be law-breakers, in the busy, stressful maelstrom of modern life there is precious little room for sympathy for or even attention to their plight.

People are also aware that the history of punishment is one of progressive softening in penal methods[119] and frequently believe that this process has gone too far. In the latter part of the last century treadmills and cranks were still in operation in Ireland. These were designed to give vigorous life to the concepts of 'penal servitude' and 'hard labour'. In other words, imprisonment in the not too distant past was deliberately planned as a brutish, crushingly punitive experience. Even William Crofton's progressive 'Irish System', which introduced the sequence of forced labour on public works, open prison, and parole as adjuncts to an initial period of solitary confinement, was described by a contemporary[120] in the following terms: 'As the convict's moral progress advances, his state of duress becomes less vile; and he is at last treated as a man and trusted as such.' Vile duress and dehumanisation were obviously a deliberate part of the project.

The movement away from these harsh methods has been, in some respects, spectacular, to the point where the declared first principle of our present penal system is to deprive liberty *as* the punishment, not *for* punishment. But in many ways the general public, in their views on the objectives of prison, lag far behind the declared, official thinking and still expect the prison regime to hurt inmates. David Garland[121] argues that: 'The prison provides a way of punishing people – of subjecting them to hard treatment, inflicting pain, doing them harm – which is largely compatible with modern sensibilities and conventional constraints upon open, physical violence.' If this is the case, if prisons are covertly designed to inflict pain because this is what the public really want, then this fact would partly explain the yawning gap between the aspiration to punish solely by deprivation of liberty and the harsh everyday reality within the prisons. Even if this is not true, the principled aim to punish only by deprivation of liberty is likely to remain an insincere, aspirational gesture so as long as large sectors of public and political opinion cling to ideas of prison as the proper site of well-deserved 'less eligible' treatment and of an *acceptable* level of harsh punishment apart from and above the mere loss of liberty.

Not all public attitudes to prisoners are negative and punitive, however, and many people feel considerable sympathy for underprivileged offenders, who end up in prison, and would wish to ameliorate their situation. But this view tends to be rooted in an attitude of charity rather than any sense of moral obligation. People normally fail to grasp the logical link between the kind of social deprivation that generates crime and their own relatively more privileged situation in society. The sense of mutual interdependence and collective responsibility for society is no longer well developed and a culture of individualism predominates in Irish society. In this context, it is difficult to convince those who have to struggle for legitimate, economic survival that 'guilt and culpability are so intrinsic in our social and cultural system that we can never blame just one person as we still do in our criminal law system'.[122]

Public sensibilities have changed, but are now complex and deeply ambivalent. Public and political attitudes exhibit some signs of progress in understanding, but still obviously retain many traces of primitive punitive thinking. People inevitably and, as I have argued, rightly look to society to punish law-breakers, sometimes with imprisonment. The penal system rightly substitutes an orderly, dispassionate system of retribution for the revenge of victims. This necessarily involves a process of condemnation and blame that, I have argued, must in the final analysis discount the role of the social environment and place the chief responsibility upon the offender himself for his crime and for the punishment he receives.

Given these realities and the mindset they engender, it is easy for people and the system itself to forget that the state has a responsibility for the moral quality of the concrete forms of punishment. 'Law and order' and 'zero tolerance' ideology also obviously chimes well with some of the thinking of the general public. However, this ideology is facile and exploitative, playing to the lowest common denominator and promoting one-dimensional, punitive thinking. It focuses solely on the deterrent value of punishment and decontextualises offending, totally ignoring the broader social conditions that generate it.

It is extremely difficult psychologically for people, who may have been irreparably harmed by offenders, to understand that society can be wrong in its pattern of treatment of offenders, especially when all individual offenders may have been correctly condemned and given the benefits of 'due process' and proportionality and the protection of the human rights machinery. It can be argued that, ironically, a normally well-grounded trust in the existing legal safeguards blinds people to the fact that these safeguards are totally insufficient to ensure that the actual means of punishment are just, humane and constructive. However, as I have argued, the cumulative effect of many individual instances of legitimate state punishment and the quality of punishment inflicted by the state are in their own right profoundly important in their implications for the nature of Irish society.

This complex web of often contradictory public and political attitudes and the underlying moral and philosophical complexities of punishment by the state, which I have outlined, create a formidable barrier to a clear understanding of the penal process and to the development of a rational response to its problems. In particular, they prevent or, at least, impede a clear understanding of the crucial importance of social justice to the ultimate legitimacy of criminal justice.

Tackling the social injustice of the penal system

I have argued that the kinds of criminal and crime that are punished or, conversely, are not punished by imprisonment, and the quality of the imprisonment we impose are some of the key features of our society. Because our criminal justice and penal system is a necessary institution for the maintenance of social order, it inevitably tends to protect the *status quo* and mainstream values and so largely reflects, and acts as a bulwark for, the structural inequalities that currently exist in Irish society. From this perspective, it can be argued, in Gordon Hawkins' words,[123] 'that the real social function of the prison is to repress deviation from middle class norms, maintain the *status quo*, and preserve an inequitable social order.'

Paradoxically, the system fulfils this negative social function as an unplanned byproduct of its essential work in the service of justice, most obviously exemplified in the protection of the weak and vulnerable. That the system has a negative impact at the level of social justice is a matter of profound concern and should be a spur to the reform both of the system and society, but it does not negate the primary purpose of the system, which is to address the way some predatory citizens (and corporate entities) abuse others.

While recognising that the pursuit of social justice can never be the first or the immediate goal of a criminal justice and penal system, I am suggesting that we have reached a point where it has become obvious and urgent that the requirements of social justice should be incorporated as an ancillary, but superordinate, goal of the system. The major task is to achieve a more just social order within society as a whole and this is fundamentally a matter for political action. However, the reform of the criminal justice and penal system should be fully integrated with and seen as an essential part of the political reform of society. The criminal justice and penal system reflects, symbolises and represents the current flawed social order. The criminal justice and penal system is the musculo-skeletal frame of society; it is essential to posture and movement. It must be allowed to undertake its basic regulatory tasks; it must fulfill its constitutive and solidarity-maintaining role. However, it is now, at this stage of our social development, possible and, indeed, essential to address social injustice through criminal justice and to thoroughly reform criminal justice according to the principles of social justice.

The search for social justice in society, which in Gewirth's terms[124] is a search for equality of generic rights – that is the social, cultural and economic rights as well as civil and political rights that we believe should be vindicated for everyone – cannot advance without reform of the social and economic system. As de Haan[125] states 'inequalities in well-being based on institutional sources have to be removed first by redistributive justice before a situation can be achieved in which equality of generic rights exist'.

It is clear that the criminal justice and penal system is currently one of the major social institutions creating inequalities in well-being. The system is focused on what Aristotle calls corrective justice as opposed to distributive justice and, in fact, inadvertently consolidates and reinforces inequalities of generic rights. It must be radically transformed so that, instead, it becomes a dynamic force for greater equality. This can never be the primary purpose of individual acts of punishment related to individual instances of offending, which are the main concern of the system, but, nevertheless, if we desire a more equal society, it is essential to address the aggregate, systemic effects of punishment and end the system's pernicious role in perpetuating inequality and, where possible, make the system a positive source of greater equality.

As I have argued, some of the most powerful evidence against our present system is that it disregards the immense amount of *invisible* crime, that is crime not related to poverty and social disadvantage. The paradox is that, if the criminal justice system was more effective against *invisible* crime, the evidence that the system is a force for greater inequality in society would be substantially weakened, or might entirely disappear, but the need for punishment and imprisonment would remain and would, indeed, be far clearer.

The injustices of the system and society at present obscure the justice and necessity of punishment by the state. The need to eradicate these injustices should not be confused with any project for the abolition of punishment, based on an idealised picture of human nature; nor does it depend on a utopian belief that a totally just social order can be readily or ever realised. The damning conclusion that the Irish penal system is a source of social injustice, rather than a partial remedy for it, does not imply that we can or should abandon the use of prison, only that we should use it more sparingly, more constructively and, above all, more fairly – so that at the very least it does not add to the structural injustices of society. This approach is premised on the view that even if we know with certainty that society will always involve structural inequalities, it is a worthy and essential political aim to sincerely attempt to create the most egalitarian society possible.

Pat Carlen[126] has produced what she calls a 'state-obligated model of punishment', which would address some of the concerns I have raised. Carlen's state-obligated model proposes that punishment be seen as a process that obliges the state on three different levels. The state must use punishment in order to provide denunciation on behalf of society, restitution on behalf of victims, and rehabilitation for offenders. She also argues that 'in order to be rehabilitated offenders would need to be convinced not only that their own behaviour had been reprehensible but also that the state's treatment of them had been just.' This model rightly emphasises the moral obligation on the state to attend to the quality and real effects of the punishment it administers. It also emphasises the multiple purposes of punishment and the need to address the psychology and perceptions of the individual offender in a way that relates individual instances of punishment to broader social structures and consequences.

In my view, Carlen's model, though it fails to give due weight to the retributive purpose of punishment, is valuable. However, because it focuses on state punishment in abstraction from the broader social context, it does not go far enough in two key areas. First, Carlen fails to stress that it is essential, if criminal justice is to be in harmony with social justice, to ensure that *invisible* crime is tackled by the criminal justice and penal system to the extent that equally harmful conduct is equally punished. Second, she fails to explicitly acknowledge that it is necessary for the penal system itself to work constructively and zealously, through the use of decent living conditions, health services, therapy, education and vocational training, to address the personal deficiencies of those prisoners, who have been born (or more truly shaped by society) for crime. Most significantly, this process should be seen as a distinct moral obligation on the state, undertaken as a matter of principle – separate from and in no way conditional on the goal of crime reduction. Society owes this kind of rehabilitation to many of its prisoners, even if it does not result in 'rehabilitation' defined as cessation from crime. Happily, experience suggests that aiming disinterestedly for the personal development of the prisoner is in fact the best possible approach to dissuading him from a life of crime[127].

The major challenge for political leaders, then, is to eschew rhetoric that incites a repressive, neglectful mindset about offenders and prisons and instead to promote progressive, principled attitudes that recognise the important potential contribution of a just, humane and constructive criminal justice and penal system to the overall quality of Irish society. This can be done without in any way compromising the state's right to hold offenders accountable, to condemn them and to punish them, but it cannot be done without challenging current punitive attitudes and educating the public on the complex practical and theoretical realities of punishment.

7. In conclusion: a better future for Irish prisons?

I have painted a relentlessly negative picture of the Irish penal system and how it is run. I have concentrated on the chaos, inhumanity, ineffectiveness and injustice of the system. I have not focused on its relative merits and successes or the many things it does reasonably well. This uncompromisingly tough, critical approach is appropriate to the examination of such a centrally important and serious process as state punishment.

Punishment is an active intervention in an individual's life that can be inappropriate, damaging and unjust in countless ways, even when it is initially justified by the offender's wrong-doing, a finding of guilt through 'due process', and the careful measurement of proportionate punishment. The pattern and cumulative effects of individual acts of punishment by the state can, as I have proposed, amount to a system that undercuts social justice and perpetuates and aggravates social inequalities. Inefficient, excessive, or unjustifiable forms of punishment and poor conditions of custody are wrong in themselves, but they can also be so gravely detrimental that rather than help reduce crime they actually increase it. It is, then, essential to apply the most demanding standards to the conduct of the state in this complex and difficult area.

Even if only a small minority of prisoners suffer cruelty, physical assault, violation of basic human rights, and uncaring or actively rejecting treatment that drives them to mental illness, drug abuse or suicide, the fact that conditions exist in the prison system that allow such examples of inhumanity is a grievous indictment of Irish society. Those who suffer deep within the bowels of the prison system – lying naked and distraught in a padded cell or taunted, denigrated and threatened by all around them – are among the most isolated, powerless, devalued and voiceless people in Irish society. They have often acted in a way that deserves forcible isolation from normal society, but sometimes they are rather pathetic and relatively harmless people merely living out a ghastly destiny, for which they were groomed by dysfunctional families, uncaring social institutions and a grossly unfair society.

Beyond the extreme cases of brutal treatment, there is incontrovertible evidence that the daily reality for the majority of Irish prisoners is marked by intolerably low material conditions, a poverty of constructive services and a deleterious psycho-social environment, conditioned largely by prison officers' preoccupation with security and the prisoners' own obsession with drugs. Together these factors engender a bleak, authoritarian, but ultimately disordered, institutional regime. This impacts negatively on the psychology of the prisoner by creating a culture of idleness, dependency, depersonalisation, minimal opportunity to exercise personal responsibility, social stigma, and profound hopelessness. It confirms the denial processes of the prisoner and encourages him to rationalise his crime and to participate ever more deeply in the criminal subculture.

The history of the Irish penal system over the last few decades is a history of mismanagement, missed opportunities, and evasion of accountability. There have been major deficits in democratic, political, bureaucratic and financial accountability. The lack of basic information on and analysis of what the system is doing has had a pernicious effect on all aspects of its operation. I have argued that the overuse of prison as a sanction is a key fact. Ireland is overly punitive in relation to both the sentence lengths imposed and the use of prison against trivial offences and minor offenders. There has been a patent failure to develop non-custodial options and to rationalise sentencing practice. But even the use of imprisonment has become irrational. Political interference and the practice of shedding on a massive scale have severed the moral connection between crime and punishment, which is, at the best of times, difficult to sustain in the prisoner's mind. When early release becomes the commonplace result of a kind of lottery, it is little wonder that imprisonment loses any value it might have had as a carefully weighed act of retribution or as a deterrent.

I have argued that beyond all the internal problems of the criminal justice and penal system, beyond the fact that the system does not work as well as it could or should, lies the extremely negative role of the system in the construction of social justice. As one Irish report[128] has put it: 'the criminal justice system, which should be just and impartial, originates from and operates within a society which is neither perfectly just nor equitable'. A very divided and unequal society like Ireland tends to be highly punitive towards the crimes of the disadvantaged but lenient and forgiving towards the crimes of the privileged. This bias persists regardless of the causative role of social division and inequality in the crimes of the disadvantaged. This core injustice which penetrates to the heart of the criminal justice and penal system should be a matter of cardinal importance for any citizen who cherishes the ideal of a more egalitarian society.

I have outlined a massive agenda for radical reform of the penal system that demands change at all levels, including most fundamentally the manner in which the benefits and burdens of society are shared. It is blatantly obvious that the new Director of Prisons and the new Prisons Board are not in a position to impact greatly on the wider political agenda for social reform. Workable solutions will only be found when all the partners in this complex social enterprise share a vision and a commitment to move together in the same direction. This will require a major shift in public attitudes and a radical transformation of political activity in the area of distributive justice as well as in the criminal and penal area.

There are, however, some signs that Irish politics are evolving in a more positively egalitarian way. The politics of community empowerment, subsidiarity, and social inclusion are playing an increasingly influential role. For example, the Partnership 2000 document[129] makes an important statement, that has significant resonances with my own argument on the need to address the relation between social justice and penality. It states:

> Social exclusion is one of the major challenges currently facing Irish society. To minimise or ignore this challenge would not only result in social polarisation, which is in itself unacceptable, but also an increase in all the attendant problems such as poor health, crime, drug abuse and alienation which impose huge social and economic costs on our society. Social inclusion will therefore be pursued not in any residual way, but rather as an integral part of this Partnership and a strategic objective in its own right.

Ministers for Justice (who are now, crucially, also the Ministers for Equality and Law Reform), government and legislators must take the lead in shaping policy. They must follow a principled, comprehensive, long-term strategy that recognises the intrinsic links between socially structured inequality and the failures and injustices of the criminal justice and penal system. They must resist the temptation to interfere, for the sake of party political, electoral advantage, with the ordered development of a better criminal justice and penal system.

In a sense, this will necessitate the depoliticisation of the area – the elimination of the kind of adversarial, bipartisan politics that has led, for example, to the recent Dutch auction over the expansion of prison places. Other countries have shown the benefits of such an enlightened approach. For instance, the Netherlands[130] considered the issue of drugs to be so critical that the various political parties agreed to work in harmony for the purpose of policy-making on drugs. Another example[131] is how the Austrian political parties agreed to grant the 1989 restorative justice reforms, in the area of Austrian juvenile justice, a twenty-years breathing space, in order that they might prove their worth in the absence of undermining criticism from the opposition. Mechanisms must also be found to involve the independent judiciary, who control the central function of sentencing, and the other players in law enforcement, in the process of planned change towards a more rational and co-ordinated criminal justice and penal system. The National Crime Forum, and the interim Crime Council and the forthcoming White Paper on crime are important indications of an evolving culture of more genuine, community-wide consultation and negotiation on crime and punishment.

The new Independent Prisons Board is one of a number of important signs that there is a growing awareness of the problems of the system and a growing willingness to tackle them. The correct rhetoric is already in place in *The Management of Offenders: a Five Year Plan*, and it is now the responsibility of the new Prisons board to give authentic substance to this aspirational form. The new Board must seek and gain independence from political interference of the clientalist, populist sort that presently vitiates the administration of the penal system. Another major objective must be reform of the role of prison officers. Some of the huge amount of money spent on prison officers should be rechanneled to better purposes – improved conditions and more therapeutic and rehabilitative services. However, an even more essential reform is the refashioning of the work of prison officers to give it a constructive, directly rehabilitative focus[132].

While the current expansion of prison places provides some opportunity to improve the conditions and orderliness of current regimes, as I have argued, this can only lead to partial improvement, if the twin problems of the counter-productive, totally inappropriate overuse of imprisonment and the underdevelopment of alternatives to custody are not addressed, and if huge resources are not pumped into improved conditions and services. There is a real danger that the expansion of prison places will merely lead to an even more punitive system. The appallingly low standards of design of the new remand prison at Clover Hill reveal the origin of this initiative in a repressive, 'law and order', political ideology rather than in any genuine desire to improve the lot of prisoners. The Council of Europe Committee for the Prevention of Torture,[133] who made a recent second visit to Irish places of detention, were so disappointed in the design of this supposedly gold standard new prison that they recommended that no more than two prisoners should ever be accommodated in the cramped and unsuitable triple cells predominating in Clover Hill. The decision to refurbish, rather than demolish and replace, the depressing and totally ill-suited Victorian prisons is also a retrograde step.

On the other hand, the new Women's Prison at Mountjoy is a real and very positive advance that provides a model of how things could be throughout the prison system. This prison has excellent facilities and is well designed, creating a safe, closed environment for (near) normal living without the accent on security and containment. Separate houses are clustered around landscaped courtyards, which provide pleasing and surprising views for people moving around the building. Educational, recreational and occupational facilities are copious and well appointed. Prisoners live in small groups with some communal areas, such as kitchen and TV room, but with their own private cells. These cells can be locked from the inside by prisoners, when they do not wish to be disturbed by other prisoners. Each cell has a separate shower and toilet area. For the first time in the Irish prison system the shower and toilet cannot be seen by officers using the peep-hole into the cell. These innovations represent gigantic steps forward towards a regime that respects the dignity and privacy of inmates. At the same time the prison provides for a degree of more normal social interaction. There is a communal dining area for main meals, a reasonable visiting area with an attached outdoor play area for children, and an institutional policy of being permeable to those members of the wider community, who can work constructively with prisoners.

The new Prisons Board must take this prison, which is based on the principles of openness, normalisation and maximisation of prisoner responsibility, as its model for the future and not Clover Hill. In fact, the aim must be that all prisoners should, in the near future, be held in conditions of at least this standard.

There are also very strong arguments for the expansion of the open prisons at the expense of the closed, high-security prisons. These prisons have been sadly neglected in Ireland in recent years, partly because the Whitaker Committee was not impressed by their potential. However, open prisons automatically implement the principles of openness, normalisation and maximisation of prisoner responsibility to a degree that it is difficult to attain within a closed prison. Denmark has shown the way in the use of open prisons, holding more than two-thirds of all prisoners in such centres. Far greater use of open prisons should be a major element in the strategy for the future development of the Irish penal system, since open prisons offer by far the best prospect for realising a system that deprives liberty *as* the punishment and not *for* punishment.

The provision of a forty-place Assessment Unit at Clover Hill is also a positive sign. This marks the beginning of the implementation of the Whitaker Report's recommendation that all long sentence prisoners should be carefully assessed on committal and should be provided with a personal developmental programme for the period of their sentence. Of course, the success of this approach will depend on the provision of adequate therapeutic, rehabilitative, occupational and educational services throughout the prison system.

There are a number of other recent positive developments that indicate that the system is slowly beginning to move in the right direction. Drugs courts are being established that will divert drug-abusing petty offenders, who are mainly involved in crime in order to feed their habit, away from prison to treatment centres. The Probation and Welfare Service already runs a similar residential treatment centre for alcohol-abusing offenders. Equally, the new Children Bill places a high priority on community-based measures intended to address the social, vocational and educational problems of young people with incipient criminal careers. Policy in the juvenile justice area is beginning to be driven by a new philosophy that stresses preventative measures, positive early intervention, and diversion from the criminal justice system. The new initiative of family-group conferences introduces a restorative, reintegrative justice approach that both addresses the needs of victims and locates the problem of juvenile delinquency within the family and the community. This kind of approach is valuable because it is more likely to promote a sense of responsibility in the offender but also because it is concerned to understand the offender and address some of the problems in his or her life that make offending more likely.

The EU-funded Integra projects, including the Connect project currently operating within Irish prisons, have introduced far more sensitive and sophisticated measures to equip prisoners for the world of work. These projects take an holistic approach, focusing on personal development and social skills as much as on training in immediately marketable job skills. They also concern themselves with the post-release situation, building contacts with employers, providing sheltered workshops and a range of support services for ex-offenders making the difficult transition from the prison to the world of freedom and legitimate employment. These pilot schemes are demonstrating the real potential for positive sentence management and the personal development of prisoners within the prison system and in the early post-release phase.[134] In a very significant gesture, the recently published government National Plan has indicated that over £40 million will be spent on developing and mainstreaming Connect style programmes in the prison system over the next seven years.

On the other side of the equation, there are even some signs that Irish society is prepared to tackle more seriously the varieties of *invisible* crime. New more rigorous legislation on crimes of dishonesty, corruption and betrayal of trust is on the way and the Moriarty and Flood Tribunals are not only exposing the seriousness of 'white-collar' crime, but helping to forge new, more severe public and political attitudes to such crime. The police have become more proactive in the area of domestic violence and attitudes to drunk-driving have hardened noticeably. Farmers who use angel dust and other previously immune categories of offenders are beginning to receive prison sentences from the courts.

The growing political culture of openness and transparency is also starting to impact on the prison system. There will shortly be an independent inspector of prisons and visiting committees no longer automatically see their task as to bolster the Minister for Justice with ingratiating reports of the splendid job the prisons are doing. There is at last a meaningful budget for research into crime and punishment and immense amounts of money have been spent to provide the police, the courts and the prison system with the latest computer technology so that they can maintain adequate databases. This should mean that in the future there will be no valid excuse for the official failure to collect and publish statistics or for the failure to provide the kind of basic information and analysis that is necessary to proper understanding of the system, adequate management and rational forward planning.

There are, then, substantial grounds for real hope that the future will bring a better penal system. Some of the elements for better management and better conditions and services are in place or evolving. The new Women's Prison provides an admirable model for how things should develop. However, the signs are mixed and there is continuing evidence that some of the fundamental problems have not been identified and confronted. In particular, the overuse of imprisonment, the excessively punitive scale of punishment and the underdevelopment of alternative, community-based sanctions need urgent attention. The poor design of Clover Hill is a stark reminder that the commitment to decent conditions and basic human rights for all prisoners is not as sincere or as principled as the rhetoric would suggest. Unfortunately, effective liaison between the various components of the system and powerful, democratically accountable structures to co-ordinate and oversee law reform and operational change in the penal system remain a pipe-dream.

Above all, there is a lack of clear thinking about the role of social inequality in crime and punishment and about the contribution of our present criminal justice and penal system to social inequality – most obviously through its failure to pursue the crimes of the powerful and privileged. There seems to be an inability in Irish society to recognise that, while it is legitimate for the courts to dispense justice without regard to the role of social disadvantage in the genesis of crime, it is wrong for the political establishment and the ordinary citizen to claim a similar exemption from addressing the social inequities that breed crime. In fact, it is reasonable to support the deliberately blinkered perspective of the courts, only if in every other way the system sincerely endeavours to eliminate social inequality and remedy its pernicious effects.

It is also essential for Irish society to acknowledge the fact that the criminal justice and penal system actively contributes to social inequality by punishing disadvantage and adversity with more disadvantage, by creating new inequalities for people obviously unable to deal with those with which they were born and by protecting inherently inequitable aspects of the *status quo*. This presents an immense political challenge and calls for fundamental reform of society beginning with and centering on the criminal justice and penal system. If criminal justice and social justice are ever to become the harmonious unity they should be, then criminal justice must cease being an instrument for the promotion of greater inequality.

Irish society must rise above the simplistic, sloganeering type of ideological politics of crime and punishment that have preoccupied it in recent years. Irish society must cease using the nasty reality of crime as a rationale for circumventing the core task of creating a more egalitarian society. As Lord Woolf[135] has eloquently pointed out:

> Throughout the developed world governments are searching for ways in which to stem what is perceived

to be a tidal wave of anti-social behaviour. Their citizens are clamouring for protection. The response of government is usually to give way to the demands for longer and more punitive punishment. Experience has demonstrated that this, far from being a cure, is not even a short term palliative. The cause of the breakdown in social behaviour is the total or partial failure of a series of relationships – the relationships which should exist among and between individuals, communities and institutions.

Relationships break down in many ways for many reasons, but it is the clear responsibility of Irish society to work to eliminate the obvious disparities and inequities in relationships between citizens that currently contribute to the genesis of crime.

In the absence of more thoughtful and progressive public and political attitudes and of a rational, informed, comprehensive strategy for the criminal justice and penal system that tackles the fundamental social justice issue, there is a real possibility that present advances will have minimal constructive impact. One thing is sure, there has never been a better opportunity for radically reshaping the penal system. Technological advances and, above all, the current, unprecedentedly buoyant state of the Irish economy mean that the country has the resources to do the job properly. The Celtic Tiger economy both highlights the scandal of continuing poverty and lack of opportunity at the margins of Irish society and provides the financial means to address these problems.

Notes

1 Garland D. (1990) *Punishment and Modern Society*, p. 292, Oxford: Clarendon Press

2 Whitaker Report (1985) *Report of the Committee of Inquiry into the Penal system*, Dublin: Stationery Office.

3 D83222 (1946) *I Did Penal Servitude*, 2nd edition, Dublin: Metropolitan Publishing Co.

4 Department of Justice (1994) *The Management of Offenders: a Five Year Plan,* Dublin: Stationery Office.

5 Durkheim E. (1983) (originally 1902) 'The Evolution of Punishment' in S. Lukes, and A. Scull (eds), *Durkheim and the Law*, Oxford: Oxford University Press.

6 This is David Garland's interpretation in 'Sociological Perspectives on Punishment' in *Crime and Justice: An Annual Review of Research* (1991) Chicago: University of Chicago Press. Foucault himself writes (in Foucault, M. [1977] *Discipline and Punish,* London: Allen Lane, p. 272) 'the prison, and no doubt punishment in general, are not intended to eliminate offences, but rather to distinguish them, to distribute them, to use them; it is not so much that they render docile those who are liable to transgress the law but that they tend to assimilate the transgression of the laws in a general tactics of subjection.'

7 Carlen, P. (1994) 'Why study women's imprisonment? Or anyone else's?' *British Journal of Criminology*, 34, 131–40.

8 Coulter, Carol (1991) *Web of Punishment: An Investigation,* Dublin: Attic Press.

9 The male forms his/him/he are used throughout the text in reference to prisoners and offenders for the sake of convenience but should be read as inclusive of her/she. The choice of the male forms, of course, reflects the disproportionate involvement of males in crime and especially in imprisonment. Sex ratios in Ireland vary considerably from about 6:1 (male: female) for people coming to the notice of the Juvenile Liaison Scheme to about 40:1 for detained prisoners.

10 Tournier and Barre (1987) 'A Statistical comparison of European prison Systems' in *Prison Information Bulletin*, 10 Strasbourg: Council of Europe.

11 O'Mahony, P. (1997) *Mountjoy Prisoners: A Sociological and Criminological Profile* , Dublin: Stationery Office.

12 Earlier survey research, such as O'Mahony, op. cit., no. 11, has indicated that a large proportion of IV drug users in prison are HIV-

positive but recent research (Alwright, S., Barry, J., Bradley, F., Long, J. and Thornton L. [1999] *Hepatitis B, Hepatitis C and HIV in Irish Prisoners: Prevalence and Risk* Dublin: Stationery Office) based on oral fluid assay of a large sample of prisoners from Irish prisons has indicated a low prevalence of HIV amongst the IV drug users of approximately 3.5 per cent. However over 80 per cent of these IV using prisoners were positive for Hepatitis C and almost 20 per cent for Hepatitis B.

13   O'Mahony P. (1992) 'The Irish Prison System: European Comparisons', *Irish Criminal Law Journal*, 2, 1, 41–54.

14   O'Mahony P., *Mountjoy Prisoners*.

15   Council of Europe (1995) *Penological Information Bulletin,* nos 19 and 20, Strasbourg: Council of Europe.

16   Garda Siochana, Annual *Report on Crime*, Dublin: Garda HQ.

17   For Irish studies on victimisation see Brewer, J., Lockhart, B., and Rodgers, P. (1997) *Crime in Ireland: 1945-1995* Oxford: Clarendon Press; Breen, R. and Rottman, D. (1985) 'Crime Victimisation in the Republic of Ireland', paper no. 121, Dublin: ESRI; O'Connell, M. and Whelan, A. (1994) 'Crime Victimisation in Ireland' in *Irish Criminal Law Journal* 4, 1 85–112; and Murphy, B. and Whelan, M. (1995) Article in the periodical, *Communique, Dublin: Garda Siochana.* For an introduction to the British Crime Survey results see Hough, M. and Mayhew, P. (1985) *Taking Account of Crime: Key Findings from The Second British Crime Survey,* London: HMSO.

18   Federal Bureau of Investigation (1992) *Crime in the United States 1991*, Washington: US Government Printing Office.

19   Digest 3, Information on the Criminal Justice System in England and Wales, 1995, London: HMSO.

20   Danish Statistical Abstract (1995) Copenhagen: Government Publications Office.

21   See Dooley, Enda (1995) *Homicide in Ireland 1972-91*, Dublin: Department of Justice; Wilbanks, W. (1996) 'Homicide in Ireland' in *International Journal of Comparative and Applied Criminal Justice* 20, 2, pp. 59–75.

22   Adler, F. (1983) *Nations not obsessed with crime,* Littleton, Colorado: Fred B. Rothman.

23   Comiskey, C. (1998) *Prevalence estimate of opiate use in Dublin Ireland during 1996*, Dublin: Institute of Technology Tallaght.

24   Garda Research Unit Report No. 10/97; Eamonn Keogh, *Illicit Drug Use and Related Criminal Activity in the Dublin Metropolitan Area*, Dublin: Garda HQ.

25   Digest 3, Information on the Criminal Justice System in England and Wales, London: Home Office, 1995.

26 Rottman, D. (1980) *Crime in the Republic of Ireland: Statistical Trends and their interpretation*, Dublin: ESRI.

27 Fahey, T. (1995) 'Family and Household in Ireland' In Clancy, P., Drudy, S., Lynch, K., and O'Dowd, L., *Irish Society: Sociological Perspectives*, Dublin: IPA.

28 See Poverty Briefing no. 6 (1997), Dublin: Combat Poverty Agency; Callan, T., Nolan, B., Whelan, B., Whelan, C., Williams, J. (1996) *Poverty in the 1990s*, Dublin: Oak Tree Press; McGreil M. (1996) *Prejudice in Ireland Revisited,* Maynooth: Survey and Research Unit.

29 Personal communication with the Governor of Mountjoy Prison, John Lonergan.

30 O'Mahony, P. (1997) 'The Drugs Culture and Drug Rehabilitation within the Prison System' in *The management of the drug offender in prison and on probation,* Dublin: IMPACT.

31 O'Mahony, P., *Mountjoy Prisoners*.

32 O'Mahony, P. and Gilmore, T.(1983) *Drug Abusers in the Dublin Committal Prisons*, Dublin: Stationery Office.

33 Personal communication in interview with various Mountjoy prisoners.

34 Mountjoy Visiting Committee Report (1993), Dublin: Department of Justice.

35 Mountjoy Visiting Committee Report (1995), Dublin: Department of Justice.

36 Whitaker Report.

37 The Committee for the Prevention of Torture and Inhuman or Degrading Treatment or Punishment (December 1995) *Report on Irish places of detention*, Strasbourg: Council of Europe.

38 Report of the Advisory Committee on Prison Deaths (1991), Dublin: Stationery Office.

39 Report of the National Steering Group on Deaths in Prisons (1999), Dublin: Stationery Office.

40 O'Mahony, P. (1989) *A Review of the Problem of Prison Suicide and Recommendations on Prevention*, Internal Document Dublin: Department of Justice.

41 Murphy, P. (1999) 'Maximising Community Safety – The Treatment and Management of Imprisoned Sex Offenders' in *The Treatment of Sex Offenders*, Dublin: Irish Penal Reform Trust.

42 American Friends Service Committee (1971), *Struggle for Justice*, New York: Hill and Wang.

43 Shaw, G.B. (1922) Preface to *English Local Government: Prisons*, by Sidney and Beatrice Webb, London: Longman.

44 See the chapter on prisons in O'Mahony, P. (1996) *Criminal Chaos:*

Seven Crises in Irish Criminal Justice, Dublin: Round Hall Sweet and Maxwell.

45   Report of Prison Service Operating Cost Review Group (1997), Dublin: Stationery Office.

46   Committee for the Prevention of Torture and Inhuman or Degrading Treatment or Punishment (December 1999), *Report on Irish places of detention*, Strasbourg: Council of Europe.

47   *The Irish Times,* 16 December 1998.

48   As reported in The Committee for the Prevention of Torture and Inhuman or Degrading Treatment or Punishment (December 1995), *Report on Irish places of detention,* Strasbourg: Council of Europe.

49   In 1992 journalist and broadcaster Vincent Browne had to initiate High Court proceedings against the Department of Justice in order to get access to the Mountjoy Visiting Committee's annual report.

50   van Swaagingen, R. and de Jonge, G. 'The Dutch Prison System and Penal Policy in the 1990s' in Ruggiero, V., Ryan, M., and Sim, J. (1995) *Western European Penal Systems: A Critical Anatomy* London: Sage.

51   Christie Nils (1996) *Problems of Imprisonment in the World Today,* Strasbourg: Council of Europe.

52   Personal communication from Wolfgang Bogensberger, 1999, Austrian Ministry of Justice.

53   Dunkel, F. (1995) 'Imprisonment in Transition: The situation in the new states of the Federal Republic of Germany', *British Journal of Criminology* 35, 1, 95–113.

54   Christie, Nils, *Problems of Imprisonment in the World Today.*

55   Messner, C. and Ruggiero, V. 'Germany: the Penal System between past and future'; van Swaagingen R. and de Jonge G. 'The Dutch Prison System and Penal Policy in the 1990s' in Ruggiero, V., Ryan, M., and Sim, J. (1995) *Western European Penal Systems: A Critical Anatomy*, London: Sage.

56   O'Flaherty, H. (1999) *Justice, Liberty and the Courts*, Dublin: Round Hall Sweet and Maxwell.

57   Bacik, I., Kelly, A., O'Connell, M., and Sinclair, H., 'Crime and Poverty in Dublin: An analysis of the association between community deprivation, District Court appearances and sentence severity' in *Crime and Poverty in Ireland* (eds, Bacik, I. And O'Connell, M.), Dublin: Roundhall Sweet and Maxwell.

58   According to figures in Murphy, op. cit., no. 36 and Digest 3, op. cit. no.17 and Pease, K. (1994) 'Cross-national Imprisonment rates', *British Journal of Criminology* 34 , 116–30.

59   Provost of Trinity College, Dublin in the 'State of the College' address 27 January 2000.

60 Interim Report of the Review Group on the Probation and Welfare Service (1998), Dublin: Department of Justice.

61 See Digest 3 op. cit., no. 17.

62 Murray, C. (1997) *Does Prison Work?* London: The IEA Health and Welfare Unit.

63 Tarling, R. (1993) *Analysing Offending, Data, Models and Interpretation*, London: HMSO.

64 Montesquieu in 1748, *Spirit of Laws* at VI 12.

65 See *What Works: Reducing Offending* (ed. James McGuire) (1995) Chichester: Wiley, especially the chapter 'What do We Learn from 400 Research Studies on the Effectiveness of Treatment with Juvenile Delinquents' by Mark Lipsey.

66 Wilkins, L. and Pease, K. (1987) 'Public Demand for Punishment' *International Journal of Sociology and Social Policy*, 7, 3.

67 Human Development Report (1999) United Nations Development Programme.

68 Tomlinson, M. (1995) 'Ireland Imprisoned' in Ruggiero, V., Ryan, M., and Sim, J. *Western European Penal Systems: A Critical Anatomy*, London: Sage.

69 Fennell , C. (1993) *Crime and Crisis in Ireland: Justice by Illusion,* Cork: Cork University Press.

70 Whitaker Report.

71 Denham Commission (February 1998) *Fifth Report of the Working Group on a Courts Commission*, Dublin: Stationery Office.

72 Proceedings of the 1998 Integra Conference (Dublin 1999) *Including Prisoners and Ex-offenders in Employment and Society*, Dublin: Integra Support Structure and WRC Social and Economic Consultants.

73 National Crime Forum (1999), report, Dublin: Stationery Office.

74 Department of Justice (1997) *Tackling Crime: A Discussion Paper*, Dublin: Stationery Office.

75 Department of Justice (1998) *Strategy Statement 1998-2001*, Dublin: Stationery Office.

76 O'Mahony, P. (1994) 'Prison Suicide Rates: What Do They Mean?' in A. Liebling and T. Ward (eds), *Deaths in Custody* London: Whiting and Birch.

77 See Moos, R. (1975) *Evaluating Correctional and Community Settings,* New York: Wiley, and Thornton, D. (1987) 'Assessing Custodial Adjustment' in *Applying Psychology to Imprisonment*, London: HMSO.

78 Irish Commission for Justice and Peace (1994) *Human rights in prison*, Dublin: Irish Bishops' Commission for Justice and Peace; O'Mahony, P.(1995) 'On Human Rights in Prison' *The Furrow* 46, 3.

79   As cited in *The Consultation Paper on Sentencing* (1993), Dublin: Law Reform Commission .

80   From a speech at the Lillie Road Centre Millenium Lectures on 'The Marginalised Child', Dublin, 26 April 1999.

81   O'Mahony, P. in *Mountjoy Prisoners* indicates that 22 per cent of prisoners in that prison were imprisoned on their very first conviction and research undertaken for the presently sitting Review Group on Juvenile Justice indicates that 27 per cent of children coming before the Dublin courts on criminal proceedings receive some kind of detention on their first conviction.

82   O'Mahony, P. in *Mountjoy Prisoners* states that comparisons with the English National Prison Survey (1992, London: HMSO) show that twice as many Mountjoy prisoners are from the two lowest socio-economic classes and half as many own their own home as English and Welsh prisoners.

83   O'Mahony, P., *Mountjoy Prisoners*.

84   Report of the Tribunal of Inquiry into the Beef Processing Industry (1994), Dublin: Stationery Office.

85   McCullagh, Ciaran (1996) *Crime in Ireland: a Sociological Introduction*, Cork: Cork University Press.

86   KPMG Stokes Kennedy and Crowley (1993) *Survey on White Collar Crime* Dublin: KPMG. In this survey of 301 of Ireland's top business companies, 120 reported that they had suffered internal frauds in the past three years but only 28 per cent of these companies instigated legal proceedings against the perpetrators.

87   Swift, J. (1709) *An Essay on the Faculties of the Mind*.

88   Braithwaite, J. (1995) 'Inequality and Republican Criminology' in J. Hagan, and R. Peterson (eds), *Crime and Inequality,* Stanford: Stanford University Press.

89   Recent reports from Irish rape crisis centres suggest that only about one third of those reporting rape to the centres go on to report to the police. This is up from 20 per cent in Dublin in 1991, according to *The Report of the Conference on Violence Against Women* 1993 Dublin: Stationery Office. Of course, an unknown number of people suffer sexual assault but do not report to rape crisis centres or the police. As Tom O'Malley points out in *Sexual Offences: Law, Policy and Punishment* (1996) Dublin: Round Hall Sweet and Maxwell, there is also very considerable attrition of cases between reporting and going to trial and conviction. O'Malley has discovered that in the years 1988 to 1991 inclusive 344 cases of rape were known to the police, proceedings were taken in only 159 cases and, at the end of 1993, there were only 70 offenders in prison convicted of rape.

90 Christie, Nils, *Problems of Imprisonment in the World Today*.

91 Bean, P. (1981) *Punishment: A Philosophical and Criminological Inquiry*, Oxford: Martin Robertson.

92 Hudson, B. (1993) *Penal Policy and Social Justice*, Basingstoke: Macmillan.

93 Mathiesen T. (1995) 'General Prevention as Communication' in A. Duff, and D. Garland (eds), *A Reader on Punishment*, Oxford: Oxford University Press.

94 Described in Freeman, D. (1964) 'Human aggression in anthropological perspective' in J. Carthy and F. Ebling, F. (eds), *Natural History of Aggression*, New York: Academic Press.

95 For some discussion of these issues, see Kelly, J.M. (1993) *A Short History of Western Legal Theory*, Oxford: Clarendon Press; T.D. Weldon (1946) *States and Morals*, London: John Murray.

96 Swinburne, R. (1989) *Responsibility and Atonement*, Oxford: Clarendon Press, p. 94, as cited in Riordan, P. (1993) 'Punishment in Ireland: Can we talk about it?' *Administration*, 41, 4, 347–67.

97 Cicero *De Legibus*, 2. 5. 11.

98 Atiyah, P. (in *Law and Modern Society* [1983] Oxford: Oxford University Press) states that 'due process' represents the most significant contribution to society by any profession.

99 Jeremy Bentham (in *An Introduction to the Principles of Morals and Legislation*, 1789) promulgated the principle that the criminal law should not be used to achieve a purpose which can be achieved as effectively at less cost in suffering.

100 Lord Wilberforce in a 1982 judgement (Raymond v. Honey 1 All E.R., 756) stated that a prisoner 'retains all civil rights which are not taken away expressly or by necessary implication'.

101 National Crime Forum (1999) report, Dublin: Stationery Office.

102 For useful introductory texts on the philosophy of punishment, see Bean, P. (1981) *Punishment: A Philosophical and Criminological Inquiry*, Oxford: Martin Robertson; Honderich, T. (1976) *Punishment: The supposed justifications*, London: Penguin; Walker, N. (1980) *Punishment, Danger, and Stigma*, Oxford: Basil Blackwell.

103 Shaw, G.B., Preface to *English Local Government: Prisons*.

104 Garland, D. (1990) *Punishment and Modern Society*, Oxford: Clarendon Press.

105 Ignatieff, M. (1978) *A Just Measure of Pain*, London: Penguin Books, p. 56.

106 As cited in Garland, D. (1985) *Punishment and Welfare*, Aldershot: Gower, p. 16.

107 For a discussion of the forms and effects of the 'three strikes and out'

legislation in the U.S. see Dubber, M. (1990) 'The unprincipled Punishment of Repeat Offenders: a Critique of California's Habitual Criminal Statute', Stanford Law Review 43, 193–240 and Currie, E. (1996) *Is America Really Winning the War on Crime and Should Britain Follow Its Example?* London: NACRO. In the case of Rummell vs Estelle, 445 U.S. 263 (1980), William Rummell was sentenced to life for a third theft, the total value of all three thefts equalling ony $229.

108 Mathiesen T (1990) *Prisons on Trial*, London: Sage, p. 169; for a cred-itable attempt at the extreme challege of arguing that rapists should not be imprisoned see Finstad, L. (1990) 'Sexual Offenders Out of Prison: Principles for a Realistic Utopia' in *International Journal of the Sociology of Law* 20, 2, pp 152–78.

109 The initiation of the 'nothing works' debate is usually attributed to the article Martinson, R. (1974) 'What works?: Questions and answers about prison reform" in *The Public Interest* 10, 22–54.

110 See McGuire, op. cit., no. 53.

111 Garland, D., *Punishment and Modern Society*.

112 Nagel, T., (1979) *Mortal Questions,* Cambridge: Cambridge University Press, p. 26.

113 For an introduction to the literature on free will see Westcott, M. (1988) *The Psychology of Human Freedom*, London: Springer-Verlag.

114 von Hayek, F. (1960) *The Constitution of Liberty* Chicago: University of Chicago Press, p. 75.

115 See, for example, Curtin, C., Haase, T., and Tovey, H. (1996) *Poverty in Rural Ireland: A Political Economy Perspective*, Dublin: Oak Tree Press.

116 The term 'less eligibility' is most frequently associated with the work of Rusche, G. and Kirchheimer, O., particularly with their economic analysis of crime in *Punishment and Social Structure,* New York, Russell and Russell (1939).

117 Shaw, G.B., Preface to *English Local Government: Prisons*, no. 87.

118 The psychologist M. Lerner (1980, *The Belief in a Just World,* New York: Plenum) has proposed the just-world hypothesis which sug-gests that, in order to make sense out of senseless events, people need to believe that the world is fair – that good people are reward-ed and villains are punished.

119 Elias, N. (in *The Civilising Process: The History of Manners,* 1938, and *The Civilising Process: State Formation and Civilisation,* 1939 in English, 1982, Oxford: Basil Blackwell) develops a theory that historically the onward progression of civilisation has engendered increasingly deli-cate public sensibilities, especially about bodily functions and physi-cal contact. This leads to the softening or concealment of nasty, brutish, physically coercive processes such as punishment.

120 Anonymous (1858) 'Irish Convict prisons', *Dublin University Magazine*, 51, 166–72.

121 Garland, D., *Punishment and Modern Society* Oxford, p. 289.

122 The quote is from Bianchi, H. (1994) 'Abolition: assensus and sanctuary' in A. Duff and D. Garland (eds), *A Reader on Punishment*, Oxford: Oxford University Press.

123 Hawkins, Gordon (1976) *The Prison: Policy and Practice*, Chicago: University of Chicago Press.

124 Gewirth, A. (1978) *Reason and Morality*, Chicago: University of Chicago Press.

125 de Haan, W. (1988) 'The Necessity of Punishment in a Just Social Order: A Critical Appraisal', *International Journal of the Sociology of Law* 16 433–53.

126 Carlen, P. (1994) 'Crime, Inequality and Sentencing' in A. Duff and D. Garland (eds), *A Reader on Punishment*, Oxford: Oxford University Press.

127 For example Vennard et al. in their review of this area report a growing consensus that the most effective interventions for addressing offending behaviour are offender needs-based programmes, designed to improve the offender's skills and problem-solving capacity and relying on behavioural techniques to reinforce improved conduct. See Vennard, J., Sugg, D., and Hedderman, C. (1997) 'The use of cognitive-behavioural approaches with offenders: messages from the research.' Part 1 Home Office Research Study no. 171, London: Home Office.

128 Irish Commission for Justice and Peace and the Irish Council of Churches (1985). *Punishment and Imprisonment*, Dublin: Dominican Publications.

129 Government of Ireland (1996) 'Partnership 2000 for Inclusion, Employment and Competitiveness', Dublin: Stationery Office.

130 'Drugs policy in the Netherlands: Continuity and Change' (1995) The Hague: Ministries for Foreign Affairs, Health, Justice and the Interior.

131 Personal communication from Judge Fenz of the Vienna Juvenile Court; also see Pelikan, C. (1991) 'Conflict Resolution between victims and offenders in Austria and in the Federal Republic of Germany' in F. Heidensohn and M. Farrell (eds), *Crime in Europe*, London: Routledge.

132 For an interesting empirical study of problems with the development of the prison officer role, see McGowan, J. (1980) 'The Role of the Prison Officer in the Irish Prison Service' *Adminisration*, 28, 259–74.

133 Committee for the Prevention of Torture and Inhuman or Degrading Treatment or Punishment (December 1999) *Report on Irish Places of Detention*, Strasbourg: Council of Europe.

134 See, for example, Proceedings of the 1998 Integra Conference,, Dublin (1999), *Including Prisoners and Ex-offenders in Employment and Society*, Dublin: Integra Support Structure and WRC Social and Economic Consultants.

135 Lord Woolf in the foreword to *Relational Justice* (1994) Burnside, J. and Baker N., Winchester, Waterside Press.

Select Bibliography

Bacik, I. and O'Connell, M (eds) (1998) *Crime and Poverty in Ireland*, Dublin: Roundhall Sweet and Maxwell.

Bean P. (1981) *Punishment: A Philosophical and Criminological Inquiry*, Oxford: Martin Robertson.

Cohen S. and Schull A. (1983) *Social Control and the State* Oxford: Martin Robertson.

Committee for the Prevention of Torture and Inhuman or Degrading Treatment or Punishment (December 1995) and (December 1999) *First and Second Reports on Irish Places of Detention*, Strasbourg: Council of Europe.

Department of Justice (1997) *Tackling Crime: A Discussion Paper*, Dublin: The Stationery Office.

Department of Justice (1997) *Towards an Independent Prisons Board* Dublin:The Stationery Office.

Department of Justice (1994) *The Management of Offenders: A Five Year Plan* Dublin: The Stationery Office.

Duff, A. and Garland, D. (eds) (1994) *A Reader on Punishment*, Oxford: Oxford University Press.

Dworkin, R. (1986) *Law's Empire,* London: Fontana.

Foucault M. (1977) *Discipline and Punish* London: Allen Lane.

Garland, D. (1990) *Punishment and Modern Society,* Oxford: Clarendon Press.

Hagan, J. and Peterson, R. (1995) *Crime and Inequality,* Calif: Stanford University Press.

Ignatieff, M. (1978) *A Just Measure of Pain*, London: Penguin Books, p. 56.

King, R. and Morgan, R. (1980) *The Future of the Prison System*, Farnborough: Gower.

Irish Commission for Justice and Peace (1994) *Human rights in prison*, Dublin: Irish Bishops' Commission for Justice and Peace.

Irish Commission for Justice and Peace and the Irish Council of Churches (1985) *Punishment and Imprisonment*, Dublin: Dominican Publications.

Kelly, J.M. (1993) *A Short History of Western Legal Theory*, Oxford: Clarendon Press.

Law Reform Commission (1993) *Consultation Paper on Sentencing*, Dublin: Stationery Office.

127

Mathiesen, T. (1990) *Prisons on Trial,* London: Sage.

McGuire, J. (ed.) (1995) *What Works: Reducing Offending,* Chichester: Wiley.

McCullagh, Ciaran (1996) *Crime in Ireland: a Sociological Introduction,* Cork: Cork University Press.

National Economic and Social Council (Main author – David Rottman) (1984) *The Criminal Justice System: Policy and Performance,* Dublin: NESC.

O'Donnell, I. (1998) *Challenging the Punitive Obsession,* Irish Criminal Law Journal, 8, 5 1–18.

O'Mahony, P. (1998) 'The Constitution and Criminal Justice' in T. Murphy and P. Twomey (eds), *The Evolving Constitution of Ireland,* Oxford: Hart.

O'Mahony, P. (1997) *Mountjoy Prisoners: A Sociological and Criminological Profile,* Dublin: Stationery Office.

O'Mahony, P. (1996) *Criminal Chaos: Seven Crises in Irish Criminal Justice,* Dublin: Round Hall Sweet and Maxwell.

O'Mahony, P. (1994) 'The Irish Psyche Imprisoned' in 'The Irish Psyche', special commemorative edition of the *Irish Journal of Psychology* (13, 2).

O'Mahony, P. (1993) *Crime and Punishment in Ireland*, Dublin: Round Hall.

Rottman, D. and Tormey, P. (1985) *Criminal Justice System: an Overview* in the Report of the Committee of Inquiry into the Penal System, Dublin: Stationery Office.

Report of the Advisory Committee on Prison Deaths (1991), Dublin: Stationery Office.

Report of Prison Service Operating Cost Review Group (1997), Dublin: Stationery.Office.

Riordan, P. (1996) *A Politics of the Common Good,* Dublin: IPA.

Ruggiero, V., Ryan, M., and Sim, J. *Western European Penal Systems: A Critical Anatomy,* London: Sage.

Tomlinson, M. (1995) 'Ireland Imprisoned' in Ruggiero, V., Ryan, M., and Sim, J. *Western European Penal Systems: A Critical Anatomy,* London: Sage.

Whitaker Report (1985) *Report of the Committee of Inquiry into the Penal System,* Dublin: Stationery Office.